THE FIRST WORLD WAR

THE FIRST WORLD WAR

Summersdale Publishers Ltd
46 West Street
Chichester
West Sussex
PO19 1RP
UK

www.summersdale.com

Printed and bound in the Czech Republic

ISBN: 978-1-84953-452-9

Substantial discounts on bulk quantities of Summersdale books are available to corporations, professional associations and other organisations. For details contact Nicky Douglas by telephone: +44 (0) 1243 756902, fax: +44 (0) 1243 786300 or email: nicky@summersdale.com.

THE FIRST WORLD WAR

A MISCELLANY

NORMAN FERGUSON

summersdale

Contents

Introduction

If there is ever another war in Europe, it will come out of some damned silly thing in the Balkans.
Prince Otto von Bismarck, 1890

In 1914 few wished for war and when it began, even fewer thought it would last as long as it did. A century after, debate still rages over whether it was a just or a futile conflict. What can't be denied is that the scale of suffering and loss – spread across Europe and beyond – ensured it would never be forgotten.

I grew up in towns where every November we gathered around the war memorials to pay tribute to those whose names were displayed in metal and stone. It is hoped that this book will, in some small way, help to keep alive the memory of the war they fought.

Author's note: Because not all information fits neatly into one year or another, each of the specific year chapters contains a mixture of general information and information relating to the year in question.

Major battles and important locations of the First World War

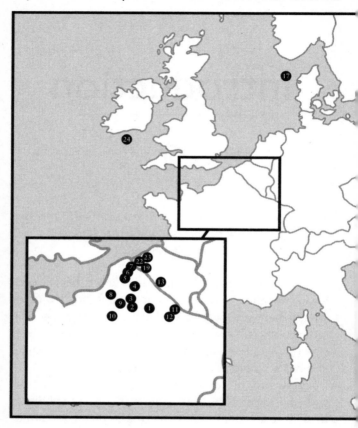

1 Marne/Peace Offensive/
   Operation Gneisenau/
   Battle of Matz

2 Aisne/Operation
   Blücher-Yorck

3 Race to the Sea

4 Cambrai

5 Arras

6 Loos

7 Neuve Chapelle

8 Somme/Operation
   Michael/Amiens

9 Compiègne

10 Versailles

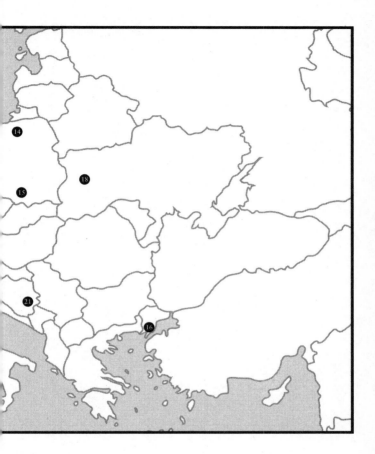

① Verdun
② Meuse-Argonne
③ Mons
④ Tannenberg
⑤ Gorlice-Tarnów
⑥ Gallipoli
⑦ Jutland
⑱ Brusilov Offensive
⑲ Messines
⑳ Battles of the Isonzo
㉑ Sarajevo
㉒ Ypres/Passchendaele
㉓ Lys/Flanders
㉔ The sinking of the *Lusitania*

Timeline

1914

JUNE

28   Archduke Franz Ferdinand is assassinated in Sarajevo.

JULY

28   Austria-Hungary declares war on Serbia.

AUGUST

1   Germany declares war on Russia.

3   Germany declares war on France.

4   German forces invade neutral Belgium.

4   Britain declares war on Germany.

4   USA declares neutrality.

6   First British casualties as HMS *Amphion* is sunk in North Sea.

6	First air raid sees nine killed as Liège is bombed by Zeppelins.
7	First British troops arrive in France.
9	Battle of the Frontiers begins as France attempts to regain Alsace and Lorraine.
12	Britain declares war on Austria-Hungary.
17	Russia invades East Prussia.
23	Battle of Mons begins as British Expeditionary Force (BEF) faces advancing German forces.
23	Japan declares war on Germany.
26	Battle of Tannenberg begins.
26	Battle of Le Cateau. Retreating British troops fight a rearguard action.
28	Battle of Heligoland Bight, the first naval engagement of the war.

SEPTEMBER

5	Battle of Marne begins.
15	Battle of Aisne begins.
22	British aircraft carry out first air raid on Germany.

OCTOBER

19	Battle of Ypres sees the Germans attempt to break through to Channel ports.
29	Turkish ships attack Russian ports in the Black Sea, heralding Turkey's entry into the war.

NOVEMBER

2	Russia declares war on Turkey.
5	Britain declares war on Turkey.

DECEMBER

3   Battle of Kolubra begins. Austro-Hungarian forces pushed out of Serbia.

8   Battle of the Falkland Islands.

16   Hartlepool, Scarborough and Whitby are shelled by German ships. 137 people are killed.

1915

JANUARY

19/20 First Zeppelin raid on Britain.

FEBRUARY

19   Campaign at Gallipoli begins with French and Royal Navy ships bombarding Turkish positions.

MARCH

10   Battle of Neuve Chapelle begins.

APRIL

22   Second Battle of Ypres begins.

25   Allied troops land at Gallipoli and face heavy Turkish resistance.

MAY

2   Germany and Austria-Hungary attack on the Eastern Front between Gorlice and Tarnów.

7   *Lusitania* is sunk by U-boat.

23   Italy declares war on Austria-Hungary.

SEPTEMBER

6   Bulgaria joins the war, signing a pact with
         Austria-Hungary and Germany.

25   Battle of Loos begins. British forces use
         chemical weapons for the first time.

OCTOBER

12   British nurse Edith Cavell is executed.

1916

JANUARY

9   Allied troops complete their evacuation from
         Gallipoli.

FEBRUARY

21   Germany launches large-scale attack at Verdun.

APRIL

29   British surrender at Kut.

MAY

31   Battle of Jutland. Only large-scale naval
         engagement of the war.

JUNE

4   Brusilov Offensive begins.

JULY

1   Battle of the Somme begins.

SEPTEMBER

15   Tanks are used for the first time at Flers-Courcelette.

DECEMBER

18   Battle of Verdun ends.

1917

JANUARY

31   Germany restarts unrestricted U-boat warfare.

FEBRUARY

9   German troops begin withdrawal to the Hindenburg Line.

MARCH

15   Russia's Tsar Nicholas II abdicates in the face of civil unrest.

APRIL

6   USA declares war on Germany.

9   Battle of Arras begins.

16   Nivelle Offensive leads to heavy losses and French Army mutinies.

JUNE

7   Battle of Messines Ridge.

JULY

6   T. E. Lawrence 'of Arabia' takes the Red Sea port of Aqaba after a surprise raid.

31   Third Battle of Ypres begins.

OCTOBER

25   Russian Bolsheviks seize power in the October Revolution.

NOVEMBER

20   Battle of Cambrai begins.

DECEMBER

11   General Allenby enters Jerusalem.

1918

MARCH

3   Russia signs Brest-Litovsk treaty with Germany.

21   Germany launches its Spring Offensive on Western Front.

APRIL

23   British attempt to block the port at Zeebrugge with sunken ships.

JULY

18   Allies begin counteroffensive actions on Western Front.

AUGUST

8   Battle of Amiens begins the Hundred Days
        Offensive.

SEPTEMBER

29   Hindenburg Line breached by the Allies.

OCTOBER

1   Damascus taken by Arab and British forces.
29   German sailors mutiny. Unrest leads to the
        German Revolution.
30   Turkey ends its involvement in the war.

NOVEMBER

3   Austria signs its armistice.
11   Germany signs the armistice document ending
        the war.

Twenty Men
and Women of
the War

ALBERT BALL

Britain's most well-known First World War fighter ace. Ball shot down 44 German aircraft and received much publicity for his aerial exploits. Aged only 19 when he went to fly at the Western Front in 1916, he was awarded the Victoria Cross after his death the following year.

VERA BRITTAIN

The British writer and peace campaigner served as a nurse in France. Her early pro-war views changed following the loss of her brother, fiancé and two close friends.

EUGENE BULLARD

The first black combat pilot. Bullard was an American who flew with the French Air Force. Later joined the French Resistance in World War Two.

JACK CORNWELL

Born in Essex, Cornwell joined the Royal Navy aged 15. He was fatally injured at Jutland but remained at his post. At 16, he was the third-youngest recipient of the Victoria Cross.

MARSHAL FERDINAND FOCH

In charge of French forces at the First Battle of the Marne. Became supreme Allied commander in 1918.

ROLAND GARROS

French pilot, whose innovation allowed an aircraft's machine gun to fire through the propeller. His aircraft was later recovered intact by the Germans, who developed the interrupter gear device for their own aeroplanes. The Parisian tennis court at which the French Open is held is named in his honour.

GENERAL DOUGLAS HAIG

Commander of British forces on the Western Front for most of war. Tactics resulting in heavy losses earned him post-war criticism.

MATA HARI

Dutchwoman Margaretha Zelle became known as an exotic dancer in Paris before the war, and adopted the stage name Mata Hari. After becoming a courtesan, she was employed by both Germany and France as a spy. Despite her role for her adopted country, she was executed by France for spying in 1917.

FIELD MARSHAL VON HINDENBURG

In charge of Germany's armed forces from 1916. Became president before handing power to Adolf Hitler in 1933.

FIELD MARSHAL KITCHENER

Became Secretary of State for War in 1914. Saw need to greatly expand the army; his face appeared on recruiting posters. Died en route to Russia in 1916 when his ship hit a mine.

T. E. Lawrence

'Lawrence of Arabia' was a British soldier who took part in the Arab Revolt against the Turks in the Middle East. His exploits in the desert became the subject of a touring show created by American journalist Lowell Thomas. Lawrence joined the RAF to escape his fame.

David Lloyd George

Effective Minister of Munitions. Became prime minister in December 1916. Keen to reduce casualties, he battled with Haig. Took a more conciliatory attitude than Britain's French allies towards Germany in peace negotiations.

General Erich Ludendorff

Responsible for the Spring Offensive in 1918 – Germany's gamble to win the war.

General John Pershing

Commander of American forces. Resisted pressure to incorporate US soldiers into Allied formations. Saw his forces make mistakes made earlier in the war by France and Britain, such as large frontal attacks, and the war ended before his true capability could be shown.

SIEGFRIED SASSOON

British Army officer awarded the Military Cross. Deemed to be suffering from 'a passing nervous shock' by a medical board after criticising conduct of the war. Wrote poems while in hospital which reflected his anti-war views.

JOHN SIMPSON

Australian, known as 'the man with the donkey', with which he helped transport the wounded at Gallipoli, where he was killed in May 1915.

KAISER WILHELM II

Germany's head of state, the Kaiser's support for Austria-Hungary was a key factor in the move towards war in 1914. Forced out of his position as emperor in November 1918.

WOODBINE WILLIE

Properly known as the Reverend Geoffrey Studdert Kennedy, this British chaplain was known for giving cigarettes to injured troops, hence his nickname. Awarded the Military Cross. Cigarettes were thrown onto his coffin in tribute.

WOODROW WILSON

US president, who, despite being elected on the slogan 'He Kept Us Out of The War', took his country into the conflict in 1917.

SERGEANT ALVIN YORK

The one-time conscientious objector York earned the USA's Medal of Honor for attacking a machine-gun postion single-handedly in October 1918.

1914

*The lamps are going out all over Europe and we shall
not see them lit again in our lifetime.*
Sir Edward Grey

FIRST SHOT

On Sunday 28 June a Bosnian-Serb student named
Gavrilo Princip shot and killed the heir to the Austro-
Hungarian Empire. Archduke Franz Ferdinand was
visiting the Bosnian city of Sarajevo when a chance
encounter gave Princip the opportunity to fire into the
open-topped car. The incident began an escalating crisis
which drew in Russia, France, Germany and Britain.
The Austro-Hungarian Empire declared war on Serbia
at the end of July.

'THE LAMPS ARE GOING OUT...'

On 3 August British Foreign Secretary Sir Edward Grey gave a speech in the House of Commons which did much to rally the country behind involvement in the war. Later that day he stood watching the lamplighters outside his London office and made his famous remark: 'The lamps are going out all over Europe and we shall not see them lit again in our lifetime.'

8.02 A.M.

At this time on 4 August, German troops crossed into neutral Belgium. As part of the Schlieffen Plan, German forces were to advance westwards through Belgium and northern France, then the right flank would swing around to encircle France's capital. The plan was intended to last no longer than 40 days, ending the war before Christmas.

'A MERE SCRAP OF PAPER'

Britain's ultimatum to Germany to withdraw its forces from neutral Belgium received no response and on 4 August war was declared. In Germany, the British ambassador met with Germany's chancellor. The chancellor expressed his disbelief that 'just for a scrap of paper Great Britain was going to make war on a kindred nation who desired nothing better than to be friends with her.'

The scrap of paper was the Treaty of London of 1839, which guaranteed Belgium's neutrality. It was signed by Austria, Great Britain, France, Prussia and Russia.

8

The number of recruits at London's main army recruitment centre at Great Scotland Yard, on 1 August. It would soon increase dramatically.

STUFT

Ships Taken Up From Trade. The War Office had prepared a very detailed itinerary of what was required to transport the army overseas should the need arise, which included every merchant vessel to be requisitioned for carrying troop and materials.

BRITISH EXPEDITIONARY FORCE (BEF)

Britain's small professional force was a fraction of the size of France, Russia or Germany's conscripted armies but was disciplined and well trained in marksmanship, a skill that would soon be required.

MESSAGES OF SUPPORT

King George V issued a message for every departing British soldier:

You are leaving home to fight for the safety and honour of my Empire. Belgium, whose country we are pledged to defend, has been attacked and France is about to be invaded by the same powerful foe. I have implicit confidence in you, my soldiers.

The Kaiser addressed his own German soldiers departing for the front:

You will be home before the leaves fall from the trees.

FIELD MARSHAL & ADMIRAL OF THE FLEET

The British military ranks held by Kaiser Wilhelm II until the war began.

THE VIGIL

The day after war was declared, *The Times* newspaper published the first war poem, entitled 'The Vigil' by Henry Newbolt. Poems became a regular feature in the paper and during August up to a hundred a day were received.

10

In the first two weeks of the war a train carrying German men and supplies to the front passed over Cologne's Hohenzollern Bridge every ten minutes.

'CONTEMPTIBLE LITTLE ARMY'

It is my Royal and Imperial Command that you concentrate your energies upon one single purpose, and that is that you address all your skill and all the valour of my soldiers to exterminate first the treacherous English and walk over General French's contemptible little army.

Reported as being issued by Kaiser Wilhelm II to his army on 19 August, there is doubt as to whether it was genuine, as no record was found in German archives and the Kaiser himself denied uttering it. Whether genuine or not, it was used as motivation: the British soldiers called themselves the 'Old Contemptibles'.

BATTALIONS* IN THE FIELD, MID AUGUST 1914

Germany	1,077
France	1,108
Belgium	120
Britain	48

(*A battalion being around 1,000 soldiers)

FIRST ENGAGEMENT

In Belgium, north of Mons, at 6.30 a.m. on Saturday 22 August a troop of the 4th Royal Irish Dragoon Guards were alerted to the approach of German cavalrymen. They mounted their own horses and gave chase. Corporal Edward Thomas fired the first British shot of the war. In a war that would see the use of advanced military technology, this skirmish also saw lances and swords being used; the British commander returned with blood on his sword. Corporal Thomas survived the war.

15

A British soldier could fire 15 aimed rounds per minute.

THE MONS TABLECLOTH

Before the Battle of Mons a group of the 2nd Battalion, King's Own Scottish Borderers, were made welcome by a Belgian family. At the end of the evening's hospitality the soldiers were asked to sign a tablecloth. In November 1918, one of the men, Major E. S. D'Ewer Coke, was in the area and remembered the incident. He was surprised when the family were still there, emerging from their battle-damaged home. They had a gift for him, something they'd kept throughout the war: a tablecloth – with all the 1914 signatures now embroidered onto the cloth. D'Ewer Coke again signed his name – the only man whose name appears twice. This unique memento now hangs in the regimental museum at Berwick-upon-Tweed.

Major battles: Mons, 23 August

In their first major battle, the BEF faced the Germans at Mons. The advancing Germans were unaware of the strength or position of the British and were unable to press home their numerical advantage. The experienced and well-trained British fought a strong defence but had to withdraw; a French withdrawal on their right flank had left them exposed.

'IT WAS ALL SO EASY'

The British soldiers' ability to sustain rapid fire – it was said German troops thought they faced machine guns – resulted in many casualties. A British NCO said later: 'Our rapid fire was appalling, even to us, and the worst marksman could not miss, as he had only to fire into the masses of the unfortunate enemy. It was all so easy.'

THE FIRST VCs

The first Victoria Cross (VC) medal of the war to be awarded to a private soldier went to Sidney Godley of the Royal Fusiliers, City of London Regiment. Godley was severely injured while operating a machine gun to help slow the German advance. At the last moment he threw the weapon into the water to prevent it falling into German hands. His citation read:

For coolness and gallantry in fighting his machine gun under a hot fire for two hours after he had been wounded at Mons on 23 August.

The first VC awarded to an officer went to Lieutenant Maurice Dease, who commanded Godley's machine-gun position. Dease was fatally injured and succumbed to his wounds at the scene. Godley was taken prisoner and survived the war.

MYSTERIES OF THE WAR:
THE ANGELS OF MONS

A fictional story published in the *London Evening News* in September told of medieval archers helping soldiers at Mons:

And as the soldier heard these voices, he saw before him, beyond the trench, a long line of shapes, with a shining about them. They were like men who drew the bow, and with another shout their cloud of arrows flew singing and tingling through the air towards the German hosts.

Months later stories started to appear of men seeing 'shining shapes', rows of archers, or angels, at the battle, although there were never any named witnesses. One soldier signed an affidavit stating he had seen a 'vision of angels'. It later transpired he wasn't even in France when the battle took place.

In 1915, Arthur Machen, the story's author, declared his tale to be fiction but it was no use – the legend had taken wings.

175

The distance in miles British troops walked in their two-week-long fighting retreat from Mons, in the blazing hot summer. The soldiers experienced shortages of water and food and were near to exhaustion – three hours' sleep in a 24-hour period was common. At times they were too exhausted to continue and turned and fought, such as at Le Cateau.

Dinant

On Sunday 23 August, in the Belgian town of Dinant, German soldiers forced worshippers out of their church. They were lined up and over 600 men, women and children were shot dead. The town was just one that experienced atrocities meted out by the invading army, who justified the killings by claiming they were rooting out *franc-tireurs* – civilian resistance fighters. Property was also targeted and at Louvain the university library was set on fire. German atrocities, both real and fictitious, were used heavily in Allied propaganda.

The Germans, by burning the library, definitely broke with wisdom and with civilization.
Rector of Louvain University

6,427

Belgian and French civilians killed in 1914 by invading German troops.

Red trousers

In an echo of earlier times, French soldiers began the war wearing bright blue tunics and red trousers. Their Cuirassier cavalrymen still wore plumed helmets and metal breastplates. Casualties were high in these early battles and more subdued uniforms were quickly introduced.

'MY GOOD LADY, GO HOME AND SIT STILL'

This was the War Office's response to Edinburgh doctor Elsie Inglis on her suggestion that women medical staff be used by Britain's armed forces. Inglis' organisation, The Scottish Women's Hospitals, eventually set up units in battle zones such as France, Salonika, Serbia and Russia. Inglis died the day after returning from Russia.

THE LUCKIEST UNLUCKIEST MAN OF THE WAR

On 22 September three elderly Royal Navy ships (nicknamed the 'Live Bait Squadron') were patrolling off the coast of the Netherlands. When HMS *Aboukir* was hit by torpedoes from German U-boat *U9*, 15-year-old cadet Kit Wykeham-Musgrave dived overboard. He was being picked up by HMS *Hogue* when that was hit. He made his way on board HMS *Cressy* and had just finished a cup of cocoa when that ship was torpedoed. Fourteen hundred British sailors were killed within an hour. Wykeham-Musgrave lived until he was 90, dying in 1989.

DORA

The Defence of the Realm Act had been passed in August. It was intended to protect military secrets but its terms widened during the war and it was used to restrict many areas of British life on the Home Front. Imprisonment without trial and newspaper censorship were introduced and amongst other powers, the government was now able to:

Take possession of land.
Take possession of any factory or plant.
Take possession of coal mines.
Clear areas of inhabitants.
Close places of public entertainment.
Close licensed premises and prohibit 'treating' (buying rounds).
Prohibit whistling for cabs.
Require inhabitants to remain indoors.
Destroy stray dogs.
Prohibit the display of lights and use of fireworks.
Restrict supply or possession of cocaine or opium.
Prohibit sexual intercourse by diseased women.

BST

British Summer Time was first introduced during the war to allow longer working hours.

Major battles: Marne, 5–10 September

My centre is giving way, my right is in retreat.
Situation excellent. I attack.
General Foch, the Marne

The Germans continued their advance but were weakened as some of their divisions were moved to East Prussia to counter the Russian threat. There was a crucial change in direction: instead of continuing westwards, to then come around behind Paris from the west, German First Army General Alexander von Kluck turned his troops to pass to the east of the capital. The Allies saw this as an opportunity to stop retreating and counter-attack.

Von Kluck realised his right flank was exposed and turned his army westwards but in doing so, opened up a large gap between him and the German Second Army, which was further to the east. The Allies exploited the gap. The Germans, not wishing to be encircled, retreated. Casualties were high, around half a million in total.

The German chief of staff, Helmuth von Moltke, suffered a breakdown after this crucial battle, which saved France from being defeated and also spelled the end of any chance of it being a short war.

The miracle of the Marne

The battle at the Marne was not a foregone conclusion and at one point French reinforcements were required urgently. To get these reserve troops forward quickly Paris taxis were requisitioned, with each vehicle transporting five soldiers to the battlefield. The French regarded the saving of the capital, and avoidance of defeat in the war, as a miracle.

25

In miles, the closest the Germans got to Paris. Forward parties could see the Eiffel Tower through binoculars. A third of the capital's citizens left and the government had temporarily moved to Bordeaux.

Major battles: Tannenberg, 26–30 August

Germany hoped the war against France and Britain would be over quickly enough for their forces to move east and defeat the Russians. The Russians mobilised more quickly than envisaged and two armies advanced on East Prussia. The Germans were outnumbered two to one. The first major confrontation at Gumbinnen on 20 August was a victory for the Russians. Things were not to go so well for the Russians in the next clash of arms.

At Tannenberg the Russian Second Army was encircled in a complete rout. The Germans had been able to intercept Russian communications and knew their battle plans in advance.

Three hundred thousand Russians were killed or wounded and 92,000 prisoners taken in one of military history's most comprehensive defeats. Russian commander Samsonov shot himself. The battle signalled the last time German territory would be occupied during the war.

Major battles: First Aisne, 15–28 September

They are waiting for you up there, thousands of them.

Royal Flying Corps pilot to troops before
the First Battle of the Aisne.

Following their defeat at the Marne, the Germans had withdrawn 50 miles north to the River Aisne. The Allies were slow in their pursuit; troops were exhausted after prolonged fighting. At one point it was thought the invaders could be pushed back into Germany but they had sufficient time to establish strong defensive positions on elevated ground to the north of the river on the Chemin des Dames ridge.

Once the British and French had made perilous crossings of the river their attacks had to be made uphill in full view of the overlooking Germans. Initial successes were overturned. Trenches were dug, a foretaste of things to come across the whole Western Front.

34

The number of men from the 1st Battalion, The Queen's (Royal West Surrey) Regiment left after the First Battle of the Aisne. They had begun the war with 1,026.

Major battles: Race to the Sea, September–October

With stalemate in place at the Aisne the war on the Western Front took another direction in what became known as the 'Race to the Sea'. Both sides tried to outflank each other in a series of engagements that ran northwards. After the German taking of Antwerp in October the remaining Belgian troops retreated westwards. Under severe pressure, they opened sluice gates to flood land to prevent the Germans' advance.

95 PER CENT

The amount of Belgian territory under German control by the end of 1914.

450

In miles, the length of the Western Front, which ran from the North Sea to Switzerland. A complicated system of trenches was dug on both sides.

180,000

Number of rifles available to Serbia's army in August, which numbered 250,000 troops. The Serbs, although outgunned and outnumbered by their Austro-Hungarian invaders, were able to mount a strong counter-attack, eventually pushing their adversaries out by December.

MYSTERIES OF THE WAR:
SNOW ON THEIR BOOTS

In August a rumour spread that thousands of Russian soldiers had been seen travelling through Britain heading to the Western Front. They were said to be definitely Russians as they still had 'snow on their boots'.

It is thought they could have been Scottish troops who wore white spats over their footwear and spoke in strong accents unintelligible to those from further south. A Lovat Scout was perhaps misunderstood after saying he was from 'Ross-shire' – close enough to 'Russia' to the untrained ear.

SHOT DOWN

On 5 October French aviators Sergeant Joseph Frantz and Corporal Louis Quénault shot down a German Aviatik using a machine gun and a rifle. The two German crew members died, the first victims of aerial combat.

Major battles: First Ypres, 19 October–22 November

The Race to the Sea culminated with the battle at Ypres. German attacks were met with strong resistance by the remnants of the original BEF and new troops recently arrived from Britain and India, alongside French and Belgian units.

At one point on 31 October the British line was breached and Ypres lay undefended. Only a rushed attack by 2nd Battalion, The Worcestershire Regiment stabilised the situation.

Casualties were high on both sides. The Germans had a high percentage of young and inexperienced soldiers known as the 'Kinderkorps' ('children's corps') – one unit suffered 75 per cent casualties. The Germans called the battle 'The Massacre of the Innocents'. On the British side the losses meant the effective end of the Old Contemptibles.

OUT OF AFRICA

After unification in 1871 Germany had expressed a desire to become an imperial nation with its own colonies around the world. This policy of *Weltpolitik* (world politics) saw Germany wanting to rival Britain with its own powerful navy and a 'place in the sun', as the Kaiser had expressed it.

At the beginning of the war, Britain was determined to defeat Germany and remove its colonies by requesting assistance from its own colonial territories. This led to a series of successes across the globe with territories in the Pacific and Asia taken. In Africa most German colonies were defeated, save for German East Africa where a small force led by General Paul von Lettow-Vorbeck used guerrilla tactics to harry his British opponents. He avoided any pitched battle where his forces would have been at a disadvantage and remained at large until surrendering two weeks after the armistice in November 1918.

'BATTLE OF THE BEES'

A British and Indian force made an amphibious landing at Tanga in German East Africa in November. Despite overwhelming superiority in numbers, the raid turned into a fiasco and the British were forced to withdraw. Angry bees attacked soldiers of both sides during the battle, hence its nickname.

2ND CAVALRY BRIGADE BEAGLES

In the winter of 1914–15 a British captain in France, Romer Williams, had a pack of hunting dogs sent over. They were given the official-sounding name of '2nd Cavalry Brigade Beagles', but hunting was forbidden by the French and they were rarely used.

THE PALS

Following Lord Kitchener's call for recruits to his New Army, men were promised if they joined up with colleagues or friends they would be able to serve together in the same unit.

The first battalions of 'pals' to form were in Liverpool and soon the rest of the country followed. Some of the battalions were:

Accrington Pals – Barnsley Pals – Birmingham Pals – Bradford Pals – Cambridge Pals – Cardiff Pals – Carmarthen Pals – Durham Pals – Edinburgh City Pals – Football Battalion – Glasgow Boys' Brigade – Glasgow Commercials – Glasgow Tramways – Grimsby Chums – Hull Commercials – Hull Sportsmen – Hull Tradesmen – Hull T'Others – Kendal Pals – Leeds Pals – Liverpool Pals – Lonsdale Pals – Manchester Pals – Newcastle Commercials – Newcastle Railway Pals – Oldham Pals – Portsmouth Pals – Preston Pals – Public Schools – Rhondda Pals – Salford Pals – Scarborough Pals – Sheffield City – South Downs – Sportsmen's – St Helen's Pals – Stockbrokers – Swansea Pals – Tyneside Irish – Tyneside Scottish

POST OFFICE RIFLES

Around 12,000 postal workers joined the Post Office Rifles battalion. Half became casualties.

75

The number of Scottish football clubs that provided recruits for the 16th Battalion, The Royal Scots, known as 'McCrae's Battalion' after its commander Sir George McCrae. One club – Heart of Midlothian – saw 11 of its players sign up on one day. In total 16 Hearts players saw active service. Seven were killed.

SRD

During the winter of 1914–15 a rum ration was introduced to British troops in the trenches. It was delivered in gallon-sized ceramic containers, marked with the letters 'SRD', for 'Service Ration Depot'. Soldiers came up with their own interpretations of what the initials stood for:

Seldom Reaches Destination
Sergeants Rarely Deliver
Service Rum Diluted
Soldiers' Real Delight
Soon Runs Dry

MINISTRY OF BLOCKADE

On 3 November Britain's Ministry of Blockade declared the North Sea a military area as part of its blockade policy, i.e. using Royal Navy ships to stop and search any ship heading to Germany. Although a successful military tactic, reducing the supply of raw materials, around 750,000 German civilians died of starvation.

CAUCASUS CAMPAIGN

On 22 December, the Ottoman Empire attacked Russia in a major offensive in the Caucasus region, in the face of which the Russians retreated. When the weather deteriorated in the mountains, an estimated 25,000 Ottoman troops froze to death without having fired a shot in anger. Instructions had been given to leave their greatcoats behind to lighten their loads. The Russians regrouped and mounted a counter-attack, whereupon the Ottomans retreated. The Ottoman Third Army had begun its offensive with 66,000 combat-ready troops. It ended with 12,000.

THE ARMENIAN GENOCIDE

Following its military catastrophe at the hands of the Russians, the Turkish leadership was keen to find a scapegoat. They blamed the Turkish Armenians: Christians who lived in an area between the territory of the Ottoman Empire and the Russian Caucasus. They were deported and many died through starvation or disease. Others were simply shot. The Armenian Genocide resulted in a possible 1.5 million deaths.

It was the happiest day of my life.

Private Adolf Hitler on receiving the Iron Cross in December 1914.
The officer who recommended him for the medal was Jewish.

LES PETITES CURIES

Polish-born radiation pioneer Marie Curie resolved to
help her adopted country (France) and worked to raise
money and equipment for 20 mobile X-ray cars, which
she also helped drive at the front. They were called
petites Curies by the French soldiers.

FIRST ATTACK

The first bomb to fall on Britain was from a German
aircraft attacking Dover on Christmas Eve. The weapon
was dropped out of the cockpit by the pilot. He was
aiming for the docks but missed and the bomb exploded
in a garden, causing one injury – to a gardener blown
out of the tree he was pruning. In total, 23 were killed
in Dover from air raids throughout the war.

*And then they sang 'Silent Night'. I shall never forget
it. It was one of the highlights of my life.*

Albert Moren, 2nd Queen's Regiment. Along with thousands of
other Allied soldiers, Moren listened enraptured as German troops
sang carols, the sound drifting across the moonlit no-man's-land.

PEACE ON EARTH

Christmas saw outbreaks of peace all along the front. Opposing soldiers mingled in no-man's-land, played football, sung carols and popular songs. In one instance, a British soldier had his hair cut by a German barber he'd known in London.

The peace wasn't to last long, being frowned on by higher command on both sides – as well as soldiers at the front such as Private Adolf Hitler, who thought it un-German – and hostilities resumed shortly after.

ITEMS EXCHANGED IN THE CHRISTMAS TRUCE

cigarettes
cigars
bread
brandy
cakes
chocolate
biscuits
tins of jam

plum puddings
sauerkraut
sausages
cards
newspapers
beer
rum
schnapps

belt buckles
uniform buttons
gloves
coins
scarves
helmets
uniforms
badges

Princess Mary's gift box

The King's 17-year-old daughter thought it appropriate that a Christmas gift box be given to every member of the services at the front or at sea. Each brass box contained:

a Christmas card
a photograph of Princess Mary
a pipe
pipe tobacco
cigarettes
a lighter
sweets*
a writing set, the pencil in the shape of a bullet*

*These were replacements for non-smokers. Indian troops received sweets and spices.

By Christmas 1914, 426,724 boxes had been given out.

First year statistics

Casualties of the major nations up until the end of 1914:

1,800,000	Russian
1,250,000	Austro-Hungarian
800,000	German
528,000	French
89,000	British

163,897

Troops in the BEF by mid September.

1,186,337

Number who enlisted in the British armed services by the end of 1914.

1915

Are there not other alternatives than sending our armies to chew barbed wire in Flanders?
Winston Churchill
Letter to Prime Minister Asquith, 29 December 1914

ZEPPELINS

The first Zeppelin air raid on Great Britain took place on 19–20 January. Great Yarmouth and King's Lynn were hit by Zeppelins L3 and L4 respectively. Four people were killed as the airships went about their mission untroubled by defensive measures. It was virtually impossible to find them in the dark and the two aircraft that did venture up both had engine failures and crash landings. One of the crew ended up thrown into a ditch full of freezing water. Several bombs fell on the royal estate at Sandringham and one of the craters was converted into a duck pond.

A SOLDIER & A WHITE FEATHER

Henry Joseph Wilding, a bombardier of the Royal Field Artillery, was charged at Highgate Police Court yesterday with causing grievous bodily harm to Arthur Houghton by striking him with his fist at High Street, Finchley, on Sunday night. He is said to be the holder of the Distinguished Conduct Medal. According to the evidence someone put a white feather in Wilding's hat and he said it was Houghton and struck him, knocking his head against a wall.
The Times, 19 January

Being handed a white feather was a sign of being regarded as a coward; many men who were wounded or on leave were given them by women and on occasions ex-servicemen would immediately attempt to rejoin the army. Badges were issued to soldiers who had been honourably discharged and also to civilians on vital war service, to prevent feathers being presented.

POSTERS

Posters were used to encourage recruitment, raise funds, and help preserve food stocks:

Daddy, what did YOU do in the Great War?
Women of Britain Say – 'Go!'
Irishmen – Avenge the Lusitania. Join an Irish Regiment today.
A call from The Dardanelles: 'Coo-ee. Won't YOU come?' Enlist now.
Your country needs you.
Remember Belgium. Enlist to-day.
It is far better to face the bullets than to be killed at home by a bomb. Join the army at once and help to stop an air raid. God Save the King.
Why are you stopping HERE when your pals are out THERE?
Lend your strong right arm to your country. Enlist now.
Turn your silver into bullets at the Post Office.
Feed the guns with War Bonds and help to end the War.
Don't waste bread! Save two thick slices every day and defeat the U-Boat.
Keep warm: you will need less food.
Eat less bread.

12.5 MILLION

War posters produced before 1916.

THE TARGET

Snipers were trained to aim for the target's teeth as, if they missed, there was a good chance of still causing an injury. If they were accurate it would lead to instant death. Snipers were a constant menace to the inattentive trench soldier and a front-line unit could expect three to four casualties each day as part of 'wastage'.

> *Do Not Stand About Here.*
> *Even If You Are Not Hit*
> *Someone Else Will Be.*
> **Western Front trench sign**

300

The number of citizens who died per day of starvation in the siege of Przemyśl. The city was in Galicia, an area then part of Austro-Hungarian territory, but now part of the territories of Poland and Ukraine. In March a final assault by the Russians took the city. One hundred and twenty thousand Austro-Hungarian troops were captured.

Major battles: Gorlice-Tarnów, 2 May–18 September

On the Eastern Front, German and Austro-Hungarian troops began their offensive between the two Polish towns of Gorlice and Tarnów. Russia's Third Army was decimated: 280,000 prisoners were captured by the end of June. Przemyśl was retaken and then Warsaw in August. Germany thought they had the war on the Eastern Front won. However, the Russians, though battered, were not completely defeated and were able to withdraw eastwards.

75 MILES

Distance advanced by German and Austro-Hungarian troops in the first week. By the end of the campaign 300 miles were gained.

Major battles: Neuve Chapelle, 10–12 March

Neuve Chapelle was Britain's first offensive action of the war. Its aims were to break through the German lines then move onto Aubers Ridge. There was French pressure on the British to show they were capable of more than just holding defensive positions.

The assault saw immediate gains. A quick artillery barrage achieved surprise and British and Indian troops of General Haig's First Army were able to take their objectives. They had a four-to-one numerical advantage over the German troops but things deteriorated as communication problems led to sluggish movement from supporting battalions. The Germans regrouped and brought in their own reserves.

The British assault had taken the small village at a cost of over 12,000 casualties. The Germans suffered similar losses.

BLIGHTY ALBERT & QUINQUE JIMMY

British nicknames for two German machine guns near Festubert.

ALCOHOL

We are fighting Germany, Austria and drink, and as far as I can see, the greatest of these three deadly foes is drink.

David Lloyd George, Minister for Munitions

There were concerns that efforts on the Western Front were being hampered through alcohol abuse on the Home Front. It was felt too much imbibing was causing absenteeism amongst war workers and with it reduced productivity.

As Minister for Munitions, and the man responsible for producing the British materials necessary to wage this total war, Lloyd George set about changing matters: he reduced pub hours, increased the duty owed and nationalised pubs and breweries. A drive to 'sign the pledge' saw King George V install a no-alcohol policy in royal households. Beer being served was made weaker and the buying of rounds was also banned.

BRITISH BEER PRODUCTION

1914	37 million barrels
1918	21 million barrels

CONVICTIONS FOR DRUNKENNESS

1914	183,828
1915	135,811
1916	84,191
1917	46,410
1918	29,075

RUM RATION

I must certainly say that had it not been for the rum ration I do not think we should have won the war.
Lieutenant Colonel J. S. Y. Roberts,
Royal Army Medical Corps

Alcohol was used to help maintain soldiers' morale and also as an incentive for those about to enter battle. It was issued daily to the troops of the participating armies to varying degrees:

Britain	–	tot of rum
France	–	¼ to ½ litre of wine or brandy
Germany	–	beer, brandy
Russia	–	none
America	–	none

375

Number of lead balls in each shrapnel shell fired by a British 18-pounder gun.

Batteries in action are not to hang their washing up in the vicinity of the guns.

Routine orders, 20 April

GUNS' NAMES

One artillery battery gave the following names to their eight guns:

Gunfire	Adder
Hellfire	Asp
Spitfire	Cobra
Wildfire	Viper

Major battles: Second Ypres, 22 April–25 May

The Second Battle of Ypres is known for being the site of the first use of poison gas on the Western Front. (It had been used by the Germans on the Eastern Front at Bulimov in January.) The chlorine gas surprised the Allies despite earlier clues, such as captured German soldiers carrying gas masks.

The greenish-yellow cloud caused panic in the lines – the French Algerian 45th Division fled. A 4-mile-wide gap was opened up into which the Germans advanced but they didn't take advantage as insufficient reserves were available. An attack the next day also used gas but the Canadians who faced it were prepared – they had been told to douse handkerchiefs in urine to counteract its effects.

By the end of the battle the Allies had lost 60,000 men in a defeat where the Germans took ground and sustained around half the Allied casualties.

168

The number in tons of chlorine gas released on the first day of the battle.

'Orace, you're for 'ome

In this manner straight-talking British General William Robertson sacked General Horace Smith-Dorrien after he suggested a British tactical withdrawal.
The British withdrew days later.

40

The British artillery barrage before their attack at Aubers Ridge on 9 May was 40 minutes long, but a lack of adequate artillery support during the attack itself led to 11,000 British casualties on the first day, with no visible success.

8,557

The number of Indian troops killed on the Western Front by the end of 1915. At Aubers Ridge, so devastating was the German machine-gun fire that no Indian troops got beyond their own trenches.

102,000

French casualties in the Artois offensive in May, where their failure to take Vimy Ridge was mirrored by the British Army's lack of success at Aubers Ridge and Festubert.

SHELL SCANDAL

An article in *The Times* newspaper in May drew attention to what it called 'a fatal bar to success' – the lack of high explosive shells. The inability of Britain to produce enough ammunition for its artillery led to the 'Shell Scandal', which brought down the Liberal government. It was replaced by a coalition.

1915 DAILY SHELL PRODUCTION FIGURES

22,000	–	Britain
100,000	–	France
250,000	–	Germany

WOMEN'S WORK

With men joining up in numbers there was a fear that productivity would go down, especially in crucial industries. Despite many reservations from employers, politicians, unions and male workers, women were employed to fill the gaps, working in such varied jobs as:

aircraft plant workers – bank clerks – bus and tram conductors – carpenters – dockyard workers – drivers – office clerks – farm labourers – instrument makers – lift attendants – lumberjacks – mechanics – mule trainers – munitions workers – nurses – police officers – postal workers – road sweepers – railway porters – taxi drivers – telephone exchange operators – train guards – typists – window cleaners

17,899

Number of British war charities set up during the war. They included:

Relief of Belgian Prisoners in Germany
The French Wounded Emergency Fund
The Serbian Relief Fund
Army Horses Fund
British Prisoners of War Food Parcels and Clothing Fund

Little Harwood Wesleyan Sunday School Soldiers Comfort Fund

Minesweepers Fund

National Federation of Discharged and Demobilised Sailors and Soldiers

The Naval Prisoners of War

The Polish Victims Relief Fund

The Russian Prisoners of War Relief Fund

The Silver Thimble Fund (which provided ambulances, mobile surgeries and hospital boats)

Major battles: Gallipoli, 25 April–9 January

The Turkish-held Dardanelles channel provided a link between the Aegean and Black Seas. It was a vital strategic objective for the Allies as its closure prevented supplies from being moved through the Mediterranean to and from Russia. A campaign was promoted by First Lord of the Admiralty Winston Churchill to secure the channel and also provide a way of reaching Constantinople and so removing Turkey from the war. It was also seen as a way of easing the pressure on Russia, which was under attack from Turkey in the Caucasus, and of giving the Allies' war new momentum away from the stalemate of the Western Front.

When British, French, Australian and New Zealand troops landed on the Gallipoli peninsula on the north of the channel they faced a tenacious and motivated enemy who had had months to prepare and dig in following abortive Allied navy raids at the start of the year.

RIVER OF BLOOD

The collier SS *River Clyde* had been converted to carry 2,000 British troops. It was to beach at Cape Helles and allow the troops to disembark through holes cut in the hull. Unfortunately it didn't make its landing point, stopping too far out. Soldiers were cut down as they left the ship in open view of the defenders. The dead and wounded turned the water red: half the men were killed within minutes.

I do not order you to fight, I order you to die.

Lieutenant Colonel Mustafa Kemal to men of the 57th Infantry Regiment. Every member of the unit was killed or wounded, and in tribute the modern Turkish Army has no such numbered regiment.

78

The percentage of men in one ANZAC battalion who suffered from dysentery. Illness caused more men to become unfit for duty than combat injuries.

ARMISTICE DAY

After a bloody Turkish attack on 19 May an armistice was arranged. Men of both sides mingled in no-man's-land to bury their dead and exchange cigarettes, bread and souvenirs, in similar fashion to the Western Front Christmas truce.

MYSTERIES OF THE WAR:
THE VANISHED BATTALION

On 10 August, 1/5th Battalion, Norfolk Regiment, landed at Suvla Bay, at the north of the western edge of the Gallipoli peninsula. Part of the force was made up of men who worked on the royal estate at Sandringham. A few days later they advanced towards the Turkish lines.

They came under heavy artillery, rifle and machine-gun fire and heavy casualties were suffered but 250 men continued under Colonel Proctor-Beauchamp. They were never seen alive again.

Reports claimed they had walked into a mysterious cloud that lifted them out of sight. Winston Churchill said it was 'without doubt the greatest unsolved mystery of this century'.

After the war a mass grave was found containing remains of soldiers wearing the badges of the Norfolk's unit. There was no paranormal explanation: they had been surrounded and killed. It was claimed some had single bullet holes in their skulls but whether these men had been summarily executed remains unknown.

He came, he saw, he capitulated.

Winston Churchill on General Charles Monro's visit to the Gallipoli battlefield in October (Monro had immediately proposed a complete withdrawal). Churchill's political career suffered in the face of the disaster he had pursued at Gallipoli and he left the government, before going on to command a battalion on the Western Front.

EVACUATION

The campaign continued into the autumn with little gained. Fresh forces landed at Suvla Bay in August and despite the way being open across the peninsula, poor command and control led to troops halting, and the opportunity was lost. In January 1916 all Allied troops were evacuated safely in a carefully planned move that surprised the Turks.

THE DEATH TOLL

Total number of troops who died at Gallipoli:

1,358	Indian
2,701	New Zealanders

8,709	Australian
10,000	French
21,255	British
86,692	Turkish

ANZAC DAY

The day of the initial landings, 25 April, became the focus of commemoration for Australian and New Zealand service personnel, with ANZAC Day still marked each year around the world.

DEATH NOTICE

On the 7th May by the sinking of the SS Lusitania, *Frank Gustavus Naumann, of 'Redhurst', Cranleigh, aged 61 years. Burial service on Tuesday, 18 May, at Saint Nicholas Church, Cranleigh at 2.45. No flowers, by request.*
The Times, 17 May

On 7 May, 1,198 died when the RMS *Lusitania* was sunk by a German U-boat off the Irish coast. Outrage ensued over this civilian ship being attacked without warning. One newspaper called it 'wholesale murder', although there was evidence the liner was carrying military supplies. Amongst the dead were 128 US citizens.

Lusitania Torpedoed By German Pirate
Daily Mirror headline, 8 May

LIVENS PROJECTOR

British Army officer William Livens vowed to avenge the death of his wife, who he thought had been killed on the *Lusitania*. Livens resolved to kill the same number of Germans as lives lost on the liner. He developed the Livens Projector, a means of launching gas cylinders at enemy trenches. When he discovered his wife was alive he still continued with his work.

ZEPPELIN DOWNED

Although in operation from the start of the war, it was not until June 1915 that a Zeppelin was finally downed. They were slow and cumbersome but not easy to shoot down, especially at night. Flight Sub Lieutenant R. A. J. Warneford, Royal Naval Air Service, attacked Zeppelin LZ37 on 7 June, his actions resulting in a Victoria Cross, the citation for which read:

This brilliant achievement was accomplished after chasing the Zeppelin from the coast of Flanders to Ghent, where he succeeded in dropping his bombs on to it from a height of only one or two hundred feet. One of these bombs caused a terrific explosion which set the Zeppelin on fire from end to end, but at the same time

overturned his aeroplane and stopped the engine.
Edinburgh Gazette, 15 June

Warneford landed behind enemy lines, repaired his aircraft and escaped safely. He was killed ten days later when his aircraft suffered structural failure.

The 'Fokker Scourge'

The period between August 1915 and early 1916 was named the 'Fokker Scourge', when Fokker Eindecker fighters caused heavy losses amongst the less agile and poorly armed Allied aircraft.

'Attack Everything'

Order posted on noticeboard by Lanoe Hawker VC, officer commanding 24 Squadron, Royal Flying Corps.

SERBIA DEFEATED

In October, Austrians, Germans and Bulgarians attacked Serbia and were able to take Belgrade. The Serbian Army withdrew and, alongside civilian refugees, retreated through the mountains of Albania. Possibly as many as 200,000 died from starvation, illness and attacks. The surviving Serbian troops (one quarter of their original force) were eventually shipped to Corfu. By the end of 1915, one in six of the Serbian population had died.

Major battles: Loos, 25 September–14 October

It will cost us dearly and we shall not get far.
General Rawlinson, commander-in-chief, IV Corps, British Army

This British offensive was to be in support of the French, who were keen to have a quick and successful offensive before winter, and to help the beleaguered Russians, bearing the brunt of German attacks in the east.

British general Douglas Haig was well aware of the difficulties facing his men: the battlefield was full of slag heaps and mine works and afforded the Germans excellent defensive positions. Despite their reluctance French commander General Joffre was adamant the British attack. Forced to act before his New Army was ready, Haig still optimistically thought a breakthrough was possible. The Allies had a five to one advantage in troop numbers.

The attack of 75,000 troops made some progress; however, it slowed due to a lack of artillery support, confusion over navigation and the heavy fire of the German defenders.

6,000

British dead on the first day at Loos. On the second day some German machine-gunners stopped firing to allow their opponents to retreat to their lines. By the end of the offensive in October British casualties were over 60,000 – triple those of the Germans.

'THE ACCESSORY'

On 25 September, poison gas (referred to as 'the accessory' for secrecy reasons) was used by the British for the first time. One of those watching was General Rawlinson:

I witnessed the sight from the top of a fosse some 3 miles distant from the front line and the view before me was one I shall never forget. Gradually a huge cloud of white and yellow gas rose from our trenches to a height of between two hundred and three hundred feet, and floated quietly away towards the German trenches. Amidst the cloud could be seen shrapnel bursting on the enemy's front line trenches.

However, the plan backfired when the wind changed direction and the gas blew back into their trenches, causing havoc amongst the British troops.

GAS, GAS, GAS

Number of attacks using gas cylinders from 1915 to 1918:
British: 150
German: 11

5,899

Despite the terror it induced, poison gas caused a relatively low number of British Army deaths during the war.

ARTOIS-CHAMPAGNE

Loos was part of the Artois-Champagne offensive, which became a dogged war of attrition, although

Allied commanders were always hopeful of achieving a breakthrough.

Artois-Champagne casualties:

British and French: 310,000
German: 140,000

Visitor attraction

A section of trench was dug in Blackpool, to help troops train for trench life. Throughout the war, for a penny a time, visitors to the 'Loos Trenches' were shown around by recovering soldiers from a nearby hospital.

The 103-hour week

In a Munitions Tribunal held in Glasgow in September, 12 apprentices aged between 15 and 18 were admonished for demanding more money. Although they were working 103 hours in a week the sheriff told them, 'No boy could be allowed to put his private wage-earning capacity in front of the national need.'

Edith

Born in 1915, French singer Édith 'Piaf' Gassion was named after British nurse Edith Cavell, who had been executed two months previously for helping Allied soldiers escape from occupied Belgium.

PLACE NAME TRIBUTES TO EDITH CAVELL

Avenue Edith-Cavell, Nice, France
Avenue Miss Cavell, St-Maur-des-Fossés, France
Cavell Corona, planet Venus
Cavell Gardens, Inverness
Cavell Gardens residential homes, Vancouver, Canada
Centre Hospitalier Interrégional Edith Cavell, Brussels
Edith Cavell Boulevard, Port Stanley, Canada
Edith Cavell Bridge, New Zealand
Edith Cavell Building, University of East Anglia
Edith Cavell car park, Peterborough
Edith Cavell Close, Thetford
Edith Cavell Day Centre, Norwich
Edith Cavell Drive, Steeple Bumpstead
Edith Cavell Public School, St Catharines, Canada
Edith Cavell Street, Port Louis, Mauritius
Edith Cavell Lower School, Bedford
Edith Cavell Ward, Homerton University Hospital, London
Edith Cavell Way, Shooters Hill, London
Mount Edith Cavell, Jasper National Park, Canada
Rua Edith Cavell, Lisbon, Portugal
Rue Edith Cavell, Brussels
The Edith Cavell pub, Norwich

'THE GARDENERS OF SALONIKA'

In October French and British troops landed at Salonika, to protect Greece from possible German attack and to assist Serbia. They arrived too late to stop Serbia being invaded and so were left in a state of limbo. More than a million troops were stationed there and given their derogatory nickname 'The Gardeners of Salonika'. The Germans called it the 'biggest internment camp'. Allied troops were involved in fighting but illness accounted for most casualties: 55 per cent of British Army fatalities were a result of disease or other non-combat causes.

LIVE AND LET LIVE

This was an unofficial policy between opposing sections of Western Front trenches that meant gunfire and trench raids would be kept to a minimum. Higher authorities were not as relaxed and issued orders that raids would be compulsory for front-line units.

TRENCH RAID WEAPONS

Trench raids saw raiding parties venturing out over no-man's-land to gather intelligence, take prisoners and generally cause havoc. Raids took place at night and men blackened their faces or wore balaclavas. They took with them an array of weapons, such as:

pistols
rifles
Mills bombs (hand grenades)
Lewis machine guns
knives (including push daggers)
knives attached to broomsticks
bayonets
knuckledusters
trench clubs (improvised with nails, metal studs)

BEEF VILLAS

British troops had their own interpretations of Belgian and French place names:

Beef Villas	Biefvilliers
Eat Apples	Étaples
Extra Cushy	Estrée-Cauchy
Funky Villas	Foncquevillers
Lousy Wood	Leuze Wood
Mucky Farm	Mouquet Farm
Monkey Britain	Monchy-Breton
Plug Street	Ploegsteert
White Sheet	Wytschaete
Wipers	Ypres

THE AFRICAN QUEEN

The inspiration for the 1935 novel *The African Queen* by C. S. Forester was an unusual battle between German and British ships on the inland Lake Tanganyika. The British had been alerted to the presence of German armed boats on the lake, which bordered German East Africa and therefore had strategic importance, as the German territory was surrounded by land controlled by Britain and Belgium.

A plan was hatched by the Royal Navy to confront the Germans, and two motorboats were laboriously transported by boat, rail, traction engine and oxen over 3,000 miles of African terrain – including a mountain range. They were moved in this way to save time in building them from crates, as was the norm for ships on the lake. The two vessels, named *Mimi* and *Toutou*, captured one German ship and sank another. A third was scuttled.

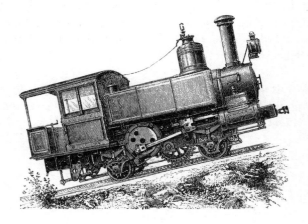

TRENCH LIFE

The British Army ensured its soldiers weren't kept in the front line for long periods, averaging four to eight days each time. They would then be rotated out to the rear areas, supposedly to rest, but were employed in training, digging trenches, laying communication lines, or carrying supplies.

3,000

Number who served as members of the Non-Combatant Corps (termed the 'No Courage Corps' by soldiers who also meted out other forms of abuse). The corps was set up in 1915 to allow those who objected to participating in the war on a combat basis to serve. They were mostly used for labouring duties. Others joined the Royal Army Medical Corps.

In this new experience you may find temptations both in wine and women. You must entirely resist both and while treating all women with perfect courtesy you should avoid any intimacy.
Message from Lord Kitchener to BEF

416,891

Total number of British Army venereal disease hospital admissions – almost six times as many as for trench foot.

378

Francis 'Peggy' Pegahmagabow was a Canadian aboriginal who served in the Canadian Expeditionary Force. He shot 378 Germans – the highest number killed by a sniper in the war.

1916

It was the most enormous disaster.
Captain Alan Hanbury-Sparrow
Royal Berkshire Regiment, the Somme

'I CAN'T GO ON.'

The last words of Private S. B. Heyes, who died of a heart attack during his period of Field Punishment Number One. Soldiers who had broken certain regulations were tied to a static object, often a gun wheel, by their hands and feet for up to two hours a day. The punishment was humiliating and it was reported that in places passing Australian troops would cut men free.

MILITARY SERVICE ACT

This act brought in military conscription for the first time in British history. From March all single men aged between 18 and 41 were eligible for call-up. (Married men were included from May and in 1918 the age increased to 51.) Exemptions applied to those who were unfit, ill, in essential jobs (such as munitions workers, miners and farmers), were ministers, or who conscientiously objected to 'combatant service'.

BLACK MARIAS, COAL BOXES, JACK JOHNSONS, WHIZZ BANGS, WOOLLY BEARS

Nicknames given to German shells.

CHOCOLATE SOLDIERS

Men of the Royal Fusiliers were thus described as they spent much of their money on confectionery.

Major battles: Verdun, 21 February–18 December

After a bombardment using a million shells, 100,000 German troops attacked the French city of Verdun. Rather than a large frontal attack, small groups of German 'stormtroopers' went forward utilising flame-throwers and grenades. The Germans gained the upper hand and took the large fort at Douaumont on 25 February without a shot being fired. German church bells were rung and a holiday granted in celebration.

The bloody battle continued through the summer and into autumn; Douaumont was recaptured almost eight months to the day after it was taken. German general Erich von Falkenhayn had claimed Verdun would 'bleed the French white' but casualties were high on both sides: the French suffered 540,000; the Germans 430,000.

After Verdun, the Germans would not undertake a large Western Front offensive for two years.

14

The average time, in seconds, between French supply vehicles passing down La Voie Sacrée (The Sacred Way) to Verdun. Two-thirds of the whole French Army took part in the battle.

Vous ne les laisserez pas passer, mes camarades.
(You shall not let them pass, my comrades.)
General Nivelle's Order of the Day, 23 June

100,000

Estimated number of troops whose remains still lie under the battlefield.

FRANCE'S COLONIAL TROOPS

France recruited men from its colonies to serve in the armed forces:

West Africans	166,000
Algerians	140,000
Vietnamese	49,000
Tunisians	47,000
Madagascans	46,000
Moroccans	24,000

Seventy thousand colonial soldiers were killed.

EASTER RISING

Irishmen and Irishwomen: In the name of God and of the dead generations from which she receives her old tradition of nationhood, Ireland, through us, summons her children to her flag and strikes for her freedom.

With these words Irish republicans stated their intentions on the steps of Dublin's General Post Office on Easter Monday. The Easter Rising, as it became known, was put down by the British Army; artillery badly damaged much of the city's centre. Over 400 from both sides were killed, including 15 leaders of the rising who were executed, which helped to engender support for their cause. The leaders wished to take advantage of Britain's preoccupation with the war and inspire a popular revolution for Irish independence. They secured German support, but the 20,000 rifles sent had been lost when the Royal Navy intercepted the vessel carrying the guns. This meant the rising was mainly limited to Dublin. Despite losing support amongst fellow republicans, the rising's leaders went ahead with their plans for a 'bloody protest'.

Kut

I have hoisted the white flag over Kut fort and town, and the guards will be taken over by a Turkish regiment, which is approaching. I shall shortly destroy the wireless.

Last message from General Townshend, Kut, Mesopotamia,
29 April

The British had begun their offensive in Mesopotamia (now mostly in Iraq) to protect oil supplies but widened the objectives to include an assault on Baghdad. Townshend had taken his British and Indian troops north up the Tigris until defeated by a Turkish force at Ctesiphon. They retreated to Kut-al-Amara where they were besieged and five months later, with relief forces unable to get through and his men starving, Townshend humiliatingly surrendered. His troops were treated appallingly with almost half dying in captivity. Baghdad was eventually taken by the British in 1917.

23,000

Casualties amongst those British Army troops attempting to relieve the besieged men at Kut.

VERY ACTIVE DUSTERS

Despite this disparaging nickname for one particular organisation – the Voluntary Aid Detachment – many organisations employed women in valuable war service:

MEDICAL

Almeric Paget Military Massage Corps
First Aid Nursing Yeomanry (Princess Royal's Volunteer Corps)
Queen Alexandra's Imperial Military Nursing Service
Queen Alexandra's Royal Naval Nursing Service
Scottish Women's Hospitals
Territorial Force Nursing Service
Women's Hospital Corps
Women's Sick and Wounded Convoy Corps
Voluntary Aid Detachment

CIVILIAN

Women's Emergency Corps
Women's Land Army
Women's Volunteer Reserve
Women's Auxiliary Force

Women's Timber Service

MILITARY

Women's Army Auxiliary Corps
Women's Forage Corps
Queen Mary's Army Auxiliary Corps
Women's Legion (Military Cookery Section)
Women's Legion (Motor Transport Section)
Women's Royal Air Force
Women's Royal Naval Service

MEDALS AWARDED TO MEMBERS OF THE FIRST AID NURSING YEOMANRY

1	x	Légion d'Honneur (France)
5	x	Croix Civique (Belgium)
17	x	Military Medal (Britain)
27	x	Croix de Guerre (France)

Free a man for sea service.
Promotional slogan for Women's Royal Naval Service.

Major battles: Jutland, 31 May–1 June

Both sides claimed victory in what was the war's only major naval engagement. Jutland saw the

Imperial German Navy attempt to strike a victory over the Royal Navy, but it was not decisive. While British losses were greater, the Royal Navy was able to continue its operations and the German High Seas Fleet mostly remained in port for the rest of the war.

There seems to be something wrong with our bloody ships today.

Vice-Admiral David Beatty, after losing HMS *Indefatigable* and HMS *Queen Mary* to German shells. After being hit the ships exploded and quickly sank.

2

Number of survivors from HMS *Indefatigable*'s crew of 1,119.

250

Number of ships in the battle.

LOSSES

	Britain	Germany
Ships	14	11
Fatalities	6,094	2,551
Wounded	510	507

SHIPS LOST

BRITISH	GERMAN

BRITISH

Battlecruisers:
Indefatigable
Queen Mary
Invincible

Armoured cruisers:
Black Prince
Defence
Warrior

Destroyers:
Ardent
Fortune
Nestor
Nomad
Shark
Sparrowhawk
Tipperary
Turbulent

GERMAN

Battlecruiser:
Lützow

Battleship:
Pommern

Light cruisers:
Elbing
Frauenlob
Rostock
Wiesbaden

Heavy torpedo boats:
S35
V4
V48
V27
V29

The only man on either side who could lose the war in an afternoon.

Winston Churchill on Admiral Jellicoe,
commander British Grand Fleet

CHEERIO, CHUM!

In one British trench the hand of a dead soldier stuck out of the wall. When troops passed they'd shake the hand and give it a hearty farewell. It was not unusual for corpses to be used in shoring up trench walls.

THE OLYMPICS

The 1916 Olympic Games were due to be held in Berlin but were cancelled. The 1920 games took place in Antwerp in honour of the suffering of the people of Belgium. The flag featuring the Olympic Rings – symbolising the universality of the games – was raised for the first time. Berlin next hosted the games in 1936.

Major battles: Brusilov Offensive, 4 June–20 September

General Alexei Brusilov, commander of the Russian forces in the south-west of the Eastern Front, formulated tactics that combined rapid movement with concentrated support fire allowing soldiers to advance quickly while avoiding heavily defended positions.

Italy, under pressure from Austro-Hungarian forces on the Italian Front, had asked for assistance and in response, along with planned French and British attacks in France, Russia launched what became known as the Brusilov Offensive. They advanced across a 300-mile-wide front, quickly pushing back Austrian and German divisions. The Germans moved troops from Verdun to bolster their allies and then fought back to regain lost territory. Austro-Hungarian armies were unable to launch their own offensives again.

While the Brusilov Offensive was initially one of the war's most successful campaigns, it came at a heavy price: the Central Powers lost 1.5 million men and the Russians half a million. These heavy casualties furthered discontent in Russia.

Major battles: The Somme, 1 July–18 November

The Battle of the Somme has become a symbol of the war on the Western Front: massed ranks of inexperienced soldiers rising out of their trenches to be mown down by machine gun or blown apart by artillery. Although intended to produce a decisive strike against the Germans, forcing a gap which British and French forces could drive through, a drawn-out war of attrition was fought, involving 12 separate battles:

Albert, 1–13 July
Bazentin Ridge, 14–17 July
Delville Wood, 15 July – 3 September
Pozières Ridge, 23 July – 3 September
Guillemont, 3–6 September
Ginchy, 9 September
Flers-Courcelette, 15–22 September
Morval, 25–28 September
Thiepval Ridge, 26–28 September
Le Transloy, 1–18 October
Ancre Heights, 1 October – 11 November
Ancre, 13–18 November

1,732,873

Number of shells used in the preliminary bombardment.

30

Percentage of British shells in the pre-battle bombardment that failed to explode.

LOCHNAGAR & Y SAP

At 7.28 a.m. on the first day of the battle, the British detonated two large mines near the village of La Boisselle. The Lochnagar mine was the bigger of the two (60,000 pounds of explosives against the 40,000 pounds in Y Sap) and it was reported by Royal Flying Corps pilot, Lieutenant Cecil A. Lewis, that the column of earth reached 4,000 feet in height.

Despite these explosions, and the week-long bombardment, the Germans' deeply dug defences and barbed wire were left mainly intact. They had heard the British tunnelling and moved their machine-gun positions accordingly.

ENTENTE CORDIALE

At the assault at Montauban, British Lieutenant Colonel Fairfax and Commandant Le Petit of the French Army advanced across no-man's-land with their arms linked on their way to taking their objective. Lieutenant Colonel Fairfax survived the war despite being gassed later that month. Le Petit was wounded in August but whether he survived the war is unknown.

THE GREAT EUROPEAN CUP

Captain Wilfred 'Billie' Nevill of the East Surrey Regiment began his company's attack by kicking a football towards the German lines as they went over the top. The ball was marked 'The Great European Cup – The Final – East Surreys v. Bavarians'. Nevill was killed minutes into the attack.

A SLOW AND METHODICAL PUSH

The day after the offensive began, a 'semi-official statement' was published in *The Times*:

The first day of the offensive is, therefore, very satisfactory. The success is not a thunderbolt, as has happened earlier in similar operations, but it is important above all because it is rich in promise. It is no longer a question here of attempts to pierce as with a knife; it is rather a slow, continuous and methodical push, sparing in lives the day when the enemy's resistance, incessantly hammered at, will crumble up at some point. From today the first results of the new tactics permit one to await developments with confidence.

47

Of the Leeds Pals battalion on the first day, 248 were killed, 267 were wounded and 181 were listed as missing. Forty-seven were uninjured.

159

The number of men from the 9th Battalion, Devonshire Regiment, killed by one German machine gun at Fricourt Wood.

5,000

Tons of ammunition being delivered each day for British guns during the offensive.

19,240

The number of British Army soldiers killed on the first day of the battle. It remains the army's highest death toll for a single day's combat. Out of the 120,000 that launched the attack, almost half became casualties.

THE BATTLE OF THE SOMME ON FILM

While the fighting was still taking place, an hour-long film called *The Battle of the Somme,* showing scenes of the actual battle (with several staged sequences), was released in British cinemas. Over the first two months of its run, an estimated 20 million tickets were sold.

The Somme was the muddy grave of the German field army and of the faith in the infallibility of German leadership.
Captain von Hentig, German General Staff

MYSTERIES OF THE WAR:
THE BLACK RAT

Private Frank Richards in his memoir *Old Soldiers Never Die* tells of how a fellow soldier was given a severe fright when confronted by a large black rat in the trenches. The soldier claimed he was doomed to die and that when he did, the rat would be nearby.

Several months later, after being transferred to the Somme, this soldier was hit by a bullet and immediately pointed to a spot in the trench where a large black rat was staring at him. The rat ran off and moments later a shell exploded. When Richards went over, he found the soldier and, lying beside him, the rat, now also dead.

British soldier's kit

Tunic, Brodie steel helmet, shirt, cardigan, cotton underwear, trousers, kilt (Scottish regiments), puttees (bandage-type coverings for the lower half of the leg), boots, greatcoat, goatskin sleeveless jerkin (replaced by leather), rifle, rifle cover, bayonet, ammunition, clasp knife, webbing, paybook, shaving equipment, toothbrush, mess kit, knife, fork, spoon, comb, soap, sewing kit, button polishing kit, field dressing, gas mask.

I am fed up carrying this bloody bird all over France.
Message attached to a carrier pigeon retrieved
at a headquarters on the Western Front.

CHAMPAGNE & CHABLIS

Some of the names given to British Mark I tanks at the
Battle of Flers-Courcelette in September, in the first-ever
use of tanks in combat:

Casa	*Crème de Menthe*
Chablis	*Daphne*
Champagne	*Daredevil 1*
Chartreuse	*Delilah*
Cognac	*Delphine*
Cordon Rouge	*Die Hard*
Corunna	*Dinnaken*
Clan Cameron	*Dolly*
Clan Leslie	*Dolphin*
Clan Ruthven	*Dracula*

3.7

Maximum speed in mph of a Mark I tank.

28

A Mark I weighed 28 tons. Inside its claustrophobic
interior, the eight-man crew endured high temperatures

and toxic fumes. Although slow and cumbersome, the tanks were a useful addition to the attacking inventory if the conditions were right.

MALE & FEMALE

Tanks that carried 6-pounder guns were termed 'males' and those with only machine guns were 'females'.

KEEP RIGHT ON

Harry Lauder was world-famous for his stage performances as the canny Scot. One of his most popular songs was 'Keep Right On To The End of the Road', which he wrote in tribute to his son John who was killed on the Western Front in 1916. John's fiancée, Mildred Thomson, never married and left her estate to the Erskine Hospital charity set up for injured service personnel in tribute.

MOUSTACHES

Command Number 1,695 of the King's Regulations read:

The hair of the head will be kept short. The chin and the under lip will be shaved, but not the upper lip. Whiskers if worn will be of moderate length.

In October the army's Adjutant-General issued an order rescinding the regulation, making moustaches no longer compulsory.

BRITISH ARMY SONGS

Fred Karno's Army
Good Bye-ee
Hanging on the Old Barbed Wire
It's a Long Way to Tipperary
I Wore a Tunic
Mademoiselle from Armentières
Never Mind
Oh! It's a Lovely War
Pack Up Your Troubles
We're Here Because We're Here (to the tune of *Auld Lang Syne*)

I am the Hun's Father Christmas
Message painted on the side of an Allied howitzer, November 1916.

BRITAIN'S WOMAN SOLDIER

In 1914 Flora Sandes went to Serbia and served as a nurse until volunteering to fight in the Serbian Army. She received their highest bravery award after being seriously injured by a Bulgarian grenade. She reached the rank of captain until being demobbed in 1922. Sandes said about her time in the army: 'I never loved anything so much in my life.' She died in Britain in 1956.

MYSTERIES OF THE WAR:
THE MONTROSE GHOST

In 1913 Royal Flying Corps pilot Lieutenant Desmond Arthur had been killed in a flying accident near Montrose. A report in 1916 had blamed Arthur for the destruction of his aeroplane, after which a mysterious figure was seen at the airfield, wearing flying gear. It would be seen walking towards the airfield's buildings, or standing beside the fire in the airmen's quarters. The apparition would suddenly disappear in front of witnesses' eyes. Word spread to squadrons on the Western Front and the authorities instigated another investigation, which exonerated Arthur. His ghost vanished.

FATHER & SON

George Lee and his son Robert served in the same artillery battery and were killed on the same day: 5 September. They are buried side by side in Dartmoor Cemetery.

18 NOVEMBER 1916

The day the battle of the Somme ended. Total casualties:

British:	420,000
French:	200,000
German:	450,000

1917

*It is impossible for us to go on with the war if losses
like this continue.*
First Sea Lord John Jellicoe, April 1917

THE U-BOAT MENACE

Although they had been used in warfare since the
eighteenth century, it was during the First World War
that the submarine, especially the German U-boat
(*Unterseeboot*), came to play a crucial role. Debate
raged in Germany over whether their submarines should
attack civilian ships without warning or conform to
'prize rules' and warn the ship's crew first. Some amongst
the German high command thought that unrestricted
submarine warfare could antagonise America to enter
the war; others reasoned it would finish the war early.

In February 1917 Germany opted to allow unrestricted
U-boat warfare. In the next three months they sank over

500 ships. It had a major effect on the transportation to Britain of supplies, leading even to the banning of rice being thrown at weddings.

New technical and tactical methods were brought in, such as convoys, Q-ships (disguised armed merchant ships) and depth charges, which could sink a U-boat while still submerged, or force it to the surface where it could be fired upon, and by early 1918 the Atlantic was safe enough to allow the huge numbers of American troops to be transported to Europe.

> *Germany is finished.*
>
> German Chancellor Bethmann-Hollweg, on the decision made by the Kaiser and the military chiefs allowing unrestricted U-boat warfare.

ALLIED SHIPS LOST TO U-BOATS

1914	3
1915	396
1916	964
1917	2,439
1918	1,035

545,282

British merchant ship tonnage lost in the most costly month: April 1917.

Convoys

25 per cent	–	Shipping loss rate before convoy system introduced.
1 per cent	–	Loss rate after its introduction.

'Turnip winter'

In Germany a scarcity of potatoes in the winter of 1916–17 led to other foods, such as turnips, being turned to for sustenance.

13

Number of ships sunk by Austro-Hungarian submarine commander Georg Ludwig von Trapp. His later marriage to his children's tutor and their escape from Nazi Germany provided the inspiration for the musical *The Sound of Music*.

Operation Alberich

In February the Germans started withdrawing to well-prepared, heavily fortified defences at the Hindenburg Line. By doing so they reduced the length of trenches they had to defend and so freed up troops no longer needed. They gave up more territory than the Allies had been able to gain in three years of warfare.

Major battles: Arras, 9 April–16 May

As a diversion from the imminent French Nivelle Offensive, British, Canadian, Australian and New Zealander troops attacked at Arras. One of the objectives was the strategically important Vimy Ridge. The first days were successful but as so often on the Western Front, the offensive slowed and was only continued for political reasons, to support the ailing French.

Hill 145

Hill 145 was the highest part of Vimy Ridge and the objective for the Canadian Corps, fighting as a complete unit for the first time. Their careful preparations, accurate artillery fire and tenacious fighting found success where other offensives had failed. In 1915, the French had lost 150,000 casualties there. On this occasion the Canadians suffered 10,000 casualties – half that of the Germans. The success was a major boost for the Allies and it had a longer-lasting effect in helping engender a feeling of nationhood amongst Canadians.

The 'Blood Tub'

Australian name for the battle at Bullecourt, which saw a casualty rate of 66 per cent.

4,175

The average number of British Army casualties for each day at Arras – the highest rate they experienced.

DOWN WITH THE WAR!

French commander Robert Nivelle had promised a breakthrough at Chemin des Dames that would finish the war. It was not to be, with the French Army suffering 90,000 casualties on the first day's fighting. Nivelle's plans had fallen into German hands and they had been able to strengthen and position their defences accordingly.

Disgruntled at yet another defeat and more lives lost needlessly, troops mutinied or deserted in over half the French divisions. The front line was left weakly defended but French commanders were able to keep the unrest secret from their allies and their enemies.

Nivelle was replaced and order restored. Forty-three mutineers were shot and soldiers were marched past the executed men as an incentive to keep their discipline.

ZIMMERMANN TELEGRAM

130	13042	13401	8501	115	3528	416	17214	6491	11310
18147	18222	21560	10247	11518	23677	13605	3494	14936	
98092	5905	11311	10392	10371	0302	21290	5161	39695	
23571	17504	11269	18276	18101	0317	0228	17694	4473	
22284	22200	19452	21589	67893	5569	13918	8958	12137	
1333	4725	4458	5905	17166	13851	4458	17149	14471	6706
13850	12224	6929	14991	7382	15857	67893	14218	36477	

The beginning of the most important telegram of the war.

Sent from German Foreign Minister Arthur Zimmermann to his ambassador in Mexico on 16 January, it promised American territories to Mexico if it entered the war on the German side. The coded signal was intercepted by British Intelligence and shown to the Americans in February. It outraged public opinion and soon after the United States entered the war.

VOTES FOR WAR

82–6	(Senate)
373–50	(House of Representatives)

Following a speech by President Woodrow Wilson, where he stated 'The world must be made safe for democracy', the US Congress voted to join the war on 6 April.

24 MILLION

The number of men who were registered for the draft in America; almost a quarter of the total population.

AMERICAN BEAUTIES & LIBERTY CABBAGE

With war declared, Americans turned against anything Germanic.

Sales of sauerkraut collapsed and it was renamed 'liberty cabbage'. Bismarck doughnuts were renamed 'American beauties' and German shepherd dogs became Alsatians. In an echo of what would happen in Germany years later, German books were taken out of libraries and burnt.

BLOODY APRIL

The Royal Flying Corps lost 275 aircraft and 207 men in April. The airmen were carrying out valuable aerial reconnaissance at Arras and, despite having numerical superiority, their aircraft were outmatched.

11

At one point in 1917, the average life expectancy in days of a British pilot.

162

Number killed in a bombing raid on London on 13 June by 26 Gotha bombers. Over 400 people were injured in the worst raid of the war. The Gothas were heavy bombers able to fly in the daytime or at night and were a bigger threat to the civilian population of Britain than the much-feared Zeppelins, which were susceptible to bad weather and presented a larger and less-defended target to British fighter aircraft and anti-aircraft artillery.

TARGET BRITAIN

Number killed and wounded in Britain in German raids during the war:

CAUSE	KILLED	WOUNDED
Aircraft	857	2,058
Zeppelins	557	1,358
Ships (shellfire)	157	634

THE BLACK FLIGHT

The Black Flight was a highly successful aircraft unit of the Royal Naval Air Service, shooting down 87 German aircraft. Each Black Flight aircraft's forward fuselage was painted black and given an individual name, such as:

Black Maria – Black Roger – Black Death – Black Sheep – Black Prince

TEN AIRCRAFT OF THE WAR

German

NAME	NO. BUILT	ARMAMENT	FIRST FLIGHT	MAX MPH	NOTES
Fokker Eindecker III	250	1 x machine gun	May 1915	87	First true German fighter, with a synchronised machine gun capable of firing through the propeller arc.
Albatros D.III	1,532	2 x machine guns	Aug 1916	107	Played major part in 'Bloody April'.
Gotha G.IV	230	2–3 machine guns + 1,100 pounds of bombs	1916	83	Took part in bombing campaign against Britain.
Fokker Dr.1	300	2 x machine guns	Jul 1917	103	Triplane, flown by 'The Red Baron' (Manfred von Richthofen).
Fokker D.VII	3,300	2 x machine guns	Dec 1917	124	Viewed as the best fighter aircraft of the war.

Allied

NAME	NO. BUILT	ARMAMENT	FIRST FLIGHT	MAX MPH	NOTES
Sopwith Triplane	147	1 x machine gun	May 1916	117	Very manoeuvrable; inspired Germany to build its own triplanes.
Bristol F.2b Fighter	3,800	2 x machine guns + 240 pounds of bombs	Oct 1916	123	The 'Brisfit' was one of the best two-seaters.
S.E.5a (Scout Experimental 5a)	5,200	2 x machine guns	Nov 1916	138	One of the fastest fighters; first British fighter to carry two forward-firing machine guns.
Sopwith Camel	5,490	2 x machine guns	Dec 1916	117	Camels shot down more German aircraft than any other type.
SPAD XIII	8,472	2 x machine guns	Apr 1917	135	Fast and strong French-built plane; flown by many Allied aces.

TOP TEN ACES

An ace was a pilot who shot down more than five enemy aircraft.

PILOT	COUNTRY	AIRCRAFT DOWNED
Manfred von Richthofen	Germany	80
René Fonck	France	75
Billy Bishop	Canada	72
Ernst Udet	Germany	62
'Mick' Mannock	Britain	61
Raymond Collishaw	Canada	60
James McCudden	Britain	57
Andrew Beauchamp-Proctor	South Africa	54
Erich Löwenhardt	Germany	54
Donald MacLaren	Canada	54

260,000

By 1917, the British Women's Land Army had over

260,000 women working as farm labourers. Their work allowed men to be released for military service.

OF WINDSOR

A royal proclamation was issued on 17 July:

We out of our Royal Will and Authority, do hereby declare and announce, Our House and Family shall be styled and known as the House and Family of Windsor.

The previous name Saxe-Coburg-Gotha arose from the marriage of Queen Victoria to Prince Albert in 1840 but it was felt insensitive for the royal family to have German names amidst a major war with that nation and with Gotha aircraft bombing London.

On hearing the news the German Kaiser, Queen Victoria's grandson, joked that he wanted to see the Shakespeare play *The Merry Wives of Saxe-Coburg-Gotha*.

LAST WORDS

'Annie.'
Unknown soldier
Somme, 1916

'Be brave, my boys.'
CSM John Muirhead
Somme, 1916

'Come on, lads!'
Lieutenant Colonel P. W. Machell
Somme, 1916

'If we have to die, let us die like men, like Die-Hards.'
Second Lieutenant Rupert Hallowes VC
Hooge, 1915

'I'm coming for you.'
Unknown soldier
Somme, 1916

'Mon Dieu!'
Colonel Émile Driant
Verdun, 1916

'Put that bloody cigarette out!'
Lance Sergeant Hector Munro
Somme, 1916

'Surrender be hanged. Stand up and fight!'
Second Lieutenant Roger Marshall
Aisne, 1914

'They got me in the stomach and it's bad.'
Lieutenant Roland Leighton
Hebuterne, 1915

PETS & MASCOTS

Baboon – Bear – Cat – Cow – Dog – Fox – Goat – Goose
– Horse – Lion – Monkey – Mule – Parrot – Rabbit

Animals kept as personal pets or unit mascots. The mascot of the Welch Regiment's 2nd Battalion, a goat named Taffy the IV, was awarded the 1914 Star because it had 'served' in France that year. Winnie, a black bear brought over by a Canadian officer, later became a much-loved attraction in London Zoo. The bear acted as inspiration for A. A. Milne for his series of books about a certain bear fond of honey.

1,700,000

Strength of British Army on Western Front in summer 1917.

Major battles: Messines, 7–14 June

The battle was a preliminary to a major offensive planned for Flanders. It began with a week-long heavy bombardment by the British before large underground mines were detonated. Troops then advanced alongside tanks, supported by closely controlled artillery. It was a major success for the British Army with the strategic Wytschaete-Messines Ridge easily taken and German counter-attacks repulsed. However, over 26,000 British, Australian and New Zealand troops became casualties.

Gentlemen, we may not make history tomorrow,
but we shall certainly change the geography.

General Plumer, eve of battle

420

Tons of explosives used in the 19 mines set off. Prime Minister David Lloyd George, who was staying in Surrey, asked to be woken early in time for 'zero hour' when the mines were to be detonated, and he heard the 'tremendous shock' at 3.10 a.m. Ten thousand German troops were estimated to have died.

MESSINES MINES

MINE	CRATER DIAMETER (FEET)
Hill 60 A – Left	191
Hill 60 B – Caterpillar	260
St Eloi	176
Hollandscheschuur No. 1	183
Hollandscheschuur No. 2	105

Hollandscheschuur No. 3	141
Petit bois No. 1	175
Petit bois No. 2	217
Maedelstede Farm	205
Peckham	240
Spanbroekmolen	250
Kruisstraat Nos. 1 & 4	235
Kruisstraat No. 2	217
Kruisstraat No. 3	202
Ontario Farm	200
Trench 127 No. 7 Left	181
Trench 127 No. 8 Right	210
Trench 122 No. 5 Left	195
Trench 122 No. 6 Right	228

16TH (IRISH) AND 36TH (ULSTER)

These two divisions, composed mainly of Irish Catholics and Protestants respectively, fought side by side when they took the town of Wytschaete. In 2007 two memorial stones were placed on either side of the road, inscribed with the name of each division and the words 'Irish comrades-in-arms'. In total around 140,000 Irishmen enlisted, with over 35,000 fatalities.

Major battles: Third Ypres (Passchendaele), 31 July–10 November

The aim of this offensive was to break through the German lines and drive northwards to the coastal ports from which German U-boats were reported to be operating and to take railway hubs.

On the first day it started to rain heavily. The bad weather continued, turning the battlefield into a quagmire; artillery fire had destroyed the field drainage systems. The battle dragged on, with Field Marshal Haig determined to persevere despite little being achieved. On 6 November the ruined village of Passchendaele was finally taken by the Canadians.

It was claimed the offensive succeeded in stopping German forces from taking advantage of French weaknesses, but at a cost many found too high. The British Army suffered 275,000 casualties for 5 miles of territory.

THE 'BATTLE OF MUD'

The mud at Passchendaele made for atrocious living conditions. If a soldier slipped off wooden duckboards into a shell hole it was difficult for him to be extricated and orders were given that men who got into difficulties were to be left. One soldier fell and was abandoned. When the platoon returned a few days later they found him, still alive but having had a nervous collapse, with the mud now up to his neck.

19

Number of times Inverness Copse changed hands.

4.45 A.M., 16 AUGUST 1917

Allied forces attack at Langemarck. Amongst the troops is Private Harry Patch of the Duke of Cornwall's Light Infantry. He survives the battle but a month later is wounded by shell shrapnel when three of his Lewis machine-gun team are killed. He returns to Britain and is convalescing when the war ends. He goes on to become the last British survivor of the trenches.

Patch refused to talk about his war experiences until he reached the age of 100, and his forthright views on the war and its futility made him a popular figure and focus of much attention. He once said, 'War isn't worth one life.' He died in 2009, aged 111.

Good God, did we really send men to fight in that?
Field Marshal Haig's chief of staff Sir Launcelot Edward Kiggell on visiting Passchendaele for the first time in November.

Major battles: Cambrai, 20 November–7 December

Cambrai saw the largest use of tanks so far in the war, with 476 Mark IVs being used by the British. Although first seen at Flers-Courcelette, Cambrai was where tanks showed their true potential. The battle incorporated new tactics: ground-attack aircraft and coordinated artillery fire ensured the advancing troops were able to move forward in a way uncommon to the Western Front. Surprise was achieved and troops broke through the Hindenburg Line, in places gaining 5 miles of territory. Church bells were rung in celebration. This was premature as initial gains were not supported and German counter-attacks reversed the successes. Casualties amounted to 45,000 on each side, but the battle gave hope to the Allies that new tactics could succeed.

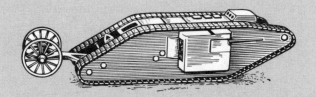

5

Mrs Amy Beechey had eight sons, all of whom served in the armed forces. Five were killed:

Barnard	–	Loos, September 1915
Frank	–	the Somme, November 1916
Harold	–	Arras, April 1917
Charles	–	Tanzania, October 1917
Leonard	–	died December 1917 after being injured at Cambrai.

When the King and Queen met Mrs Beechey, she told the Queen: 'I did not give them willingly.' Of her three other sons, Chris suffered severe injuries after being hit by a sniper at Gallipoli, Samuel served in France at the very end of the war, and Eric became a dentist in the Royal Army Medical Corps.

96

The number of British munitions workers who died in 1916 and 1917 from poisoning caused by working with TNT. Women munitions workers became known as 'canaries' due to the toxicity affecting the liver and causing jaundice.

70 PER CENT

Percentage of Britain's Gross National Product spent on war in 1917.

> *At war the penalty for not killing is death;*
> *in peace the penalty for killing is death.*
> Lance Corporal Kenneth Foster, Canadian Corps,
> member of firing squad that executed a deserter.

DEATH SENTENCES

Over 3,000 British Army soldiers were sentenced to death after courts martial, with 346 of them facing firing squads. The men were found guilty of these offences:

Desertion	–	266
Murder	–	37
Cowardice	–	18
Leaving post	–	7
Striking superior	–	5
Disobedience	–	5
Mutiny	–	4
Throwing away weapon	–	2
Sleeping	–	2

TRENCH NAMES

Trenches were given names to make navigation easier. Around 10,000 trenches and other features were named.

These are just 50:

Argument Trench
Artillery Lane
Balloon Avenue
Bumble Trench
Cemetery Trench
Cheesecake Trench
Crucifix Trench
Dead Cow Farm
Death Valley
Emu Alley
Enfilade Trench
Epicure Alley
Flapper Trench
Fleet Street
Gangrene Alley
Happy Valley
Hellfire Corner
Hiccup Trench
Hilda Trench
Hopeless Street
Hunter Street
Idiot Street
Immodest Lane
Impotent Avenue
Jelly Trench

Jock's Lodge
Joy Trench
Lager Alley
Leith Walk
Little Bear Trench
Mouse Trap Farm
Nonsense Trench
Norman Trench
Panmuir Street
Pie Alley
Pest Trench
Pompadour Trench
Popoff Lane
Princes Street
Pub Street
Racket Trench
Rainbow Trench
Rat Alley
Sandy Trench
Sauchiehall Street
Unbearable Trench
Waste Trench
Wee Trench
Whisky Corner
Why Trench

PEACE, BREAD AND LAND

This was what the Bolsheviks promised the Russian people in the October Revolution. Protests had led to the end of the tsar's rule in March, after which the Provisional Government had kept Russia in the conflict. The minister of war Alexander Kerensky advocated a fresh attack but the lacklustre Kerensky Offensive in June – although initially successful – saw the Russian Army disintegrate as the Germans overwhelmed their opponents, reaching Riga in September.

When Vladimir Lenin established the Bolsheviks as the dominant group in December, he would take Russia out of the war.

1ST WOMEN'S BATTALION OF DEATH

This Russian unit was set up to shame male Russian soldiers into fighting, however they were antagonistic towards those seeking to prolong the war. In total, 700 Russian women took part in combat.

Major battles: Battles of the Isonzo, June–November

Twelve Battles of the Isonzo were fought on the Italian Front between June 1915 and November

1917. The Italians had little success after joining the war on the Allied side and suffered heavy losses from the Austro-Hungarian forces.

Stop, go back! We won't shoot any more!
Austro-Hungarian machine-gunners to Italian troops.

1 IN 10

Italian commander Luigi Cadorna punished what he saw as underperforming units by shooting every tenth man, in a throwback to the Roman system of 'decimation'.

15 MILES FROM VENICE

German troops bolstered their Austro-Hungarian allies and together they advanced to positions 15 miles from Venice following their overwhelming victory at Caporetto in October and November. The Italians stopped their 70-mile-long retreat at the River Piave where they were reinforced by French and British forces.

260,000

Number of Italian soldiers who surrendered after Caporetto.

THE FALL OF JERUSALEM

*The capture of Jerusalem has been in some degree
delayed in consequence of the great care which has
been taken to avoid damage to sacred places in and
around the city.*

Andrew Bonar Law, Chancellor of the Exchequer, 11 December

The taking of Jerusalem was part of the campaign
to defeat Turkey in the Middle East and the British
achievement in capturing this symbolic location was a
great boost for the Allies. The ancient city was under
Christian control for the first time in 600 years.

RUSSIAN ARMISTICE

On 16 December the Russians agreed an armistice with
Germany, Austria-Hungary, Bulgaria and Turkey, thus
ending their involvement in the war. The Bolsheviks,
led by Lenin (who was given safe passage to Russia by
Germany), had achieved their aim of ending Russia's
war.

The defeat of Russia meant Germany would no longer
be fighting on two fronts and so troops were released
to take part in the Spring Offensive – Germany's last
chance to win the war.

1918

*We must strike at the earliest moment... before the
Americans can throw strong forces into the scale. We
must beat the British.*

General Erich Ludendorff, November 1917

THE CASTLE GUN

This letter appeared in *The Scotsman* newspaper on 14
January 1918:

Sir,
*Might I suggest that you would be doing a public
service if you could induce the authorities to relieve the
peaceful inhabitants of the city from the diurnal shock
of the One O'clock Castle Gun? At the present time it
is all the more an intrusion in that there are so many
convalescent soldiers within range of the concussion.
Two of these from Craiglockhart, suffering from shell*

*shock, had to be carried home from Princes Street the
other day after the shot was fired. We abolish police
whistles in the vicinity of hospitals, why keep up this
more violent reminder of their sufferings?*
I am, etc,
Citizen.

'Shell shock' was the common name given for a range of
emotional and mental disorders suffered by troops. The
symptoms included hysteria, anxiety, physical tremors,
sensitivity to noise, and nightmares.

Edinburgh's Craiglockhart War Hospital treated
soldiers suffering from shell shock; it was where
Siegfried Sassoon met Wilfred Owen and encouraged
him in his poetry writing.

The firing of Edinburgh's One O'clock Gun was
halted in April and it remained silent for over a year.

'A VERY DESPICABLE OFFENCE'

The historian and philosopher Bertrand Russell was
jailed for six months in February for writing an article
criticising the US Army. His action was described by
the judge as being 'a very despicable offence' and in
contravention of the Defence of the Realm Act as it was
likely to 'prejudice His Majesty's relations with the USA'.

HOARDING

In February, William MacCaw MP was found
guilty of hoarding the following foodstuffs. For this

contravention of the 1917 Food Hoarding Order he was fined £400.

Flour	435 pounds
Rice	134½ pounds
Biscuits	100½ pounds
Sugar	102 pounds
Tapioca	64½ pounds
Oatmeal	59 pounds
Semolina	53½ pounds
Tea	53 pounds
Golden syrup	34 pounds
Honey	21½ pounds

RATIONS

Items subject to rationing controls in 1918:

Bacon	Lard
Butter	Margarine
Cheese	Meat
Ham	Sugar
Jam	Tea

40 MILLION

Number of adult rationing books printed in June 1918.

*We had but no doubt that the great plan
would succeed.*
Lieutenant Ernst Jünger, 73rd Hanoverian Regiment

192 v. 165

German divisions facing Allied divisions on the Western Front on 21 March.

Major battles: Operation Michael / Second Battle of the Somme, 21 March–5 April

The Germans attempted to win the war with their Spring Offensive, of which Operation Michael was the first part. Reinforced with 500,000 troops from the Eastern Front, they made strong breakthroughs using gas, artillery, airpower and shock troops to bypass defensive positions in foggy conditions that hampered the defenders.

German schools were closed to allow celebrations but it was premature. Allied reinforcements were rushed in while hungry German troops slowed, gorging on appropriated food and drink.

In their advance the Germans had outstretched their supply lines and losses of over a quarter of a million casualties couldn't be sustained, so the offensive was halted.

1 MILLION

Number of shells fired in the 5-hour bombardment to begin Operation Michael.

21,000

Number of prisoners taken on the first day as the Germans overran British positions.

50 MILES

The size of the gap created in the Allied line.

CAREY'S FORCE

In the face of the German advance, General Carey was given the task of organising a last-ditch defensive unit to be positioned at Hamel, to protect Amiens. As well as infantry stragglers, 'Carey's Force' was composed of an assorted collection of soldiers, most of whom were not well versed in infantry tactics. The 3,500 men included:

artillery gunners – officers' batmen – cooks – dismounted cavalry – drivers – engineers – kitchen staff – railway troops – signallers – storemen – sappers – tunnellers

THE PÉRONNE HANDICAP

Name given to the race by the 17th Battalion, King's Royal Rifle Corps to reach the French town of Péronne before being caught by pursuing German forces.

LONG-RANGE ATTACKS

The Germans sent forward large Krupp cannons, capable of long-range firing – their shells could hit Paris from 75 miles away. The huge shells were in the air for 3½ minutes. One hundred and eighty-three hit the French capital, killing over 250 Parisians.

46/56

Forty-six of the British Expeditionary Force's 56 divisions took part in the battle.

IRON CROSS WITH GOLDEN RAYS

For his role in the success, German commander Paul von Hindenburg was awarded this, the highest medal available. The only previous recipient was Field Marshal von Blücher, for his part in defeating Napoleon in 1815 at Waterloo.

Major battles: Operation Georgette / Battle of Lys / Fourth Battle of Ypres, 9–29 April

In their second major offensive the Germans drove for Ypres and the chance to reach the important Channel ports. Depleted British units which had been involved in the fighting the previous month were stationed on what was seen as a 'quiet sector'. Portuguese troops who were in the line were under strength and lacking in motivation; a third became casualties as the Germans broke through. Allied reserves were hastily moved to stem the tide. The defence proved resolute and German commanders called off their offensive at the end of the month.

HAIG'S ORDER OF THE DAY

With the Allies under severe threat by the onslaught, British commander Douglas Haig issued a famous order on 11 April:

There is no other course open to us but to fight it out. Every position must be held to the last man: there must be no retirement. With our backs to the wall and believing in the justice of our cause each one of us must fight on to the end.

ARMED TORTOISES

Description of German tanks seen on 24 April at Villers-Bretonneux by Lieutenant Frank Mitchell of the British Tank Corps. The very first tank v. tank battle took place when three British Mark IVs faced three German A7Vs. The British were the victors in this historic engagement.

THEY WORE GAS MASKS

The renowned Australian Corps came under the command of the British Army's General Rawlinson in early 1918. He was pleased with the men and wrote in his diary:

They are certainly original fighters and up to all sorts of dodges, some of which would shock a strict disciplinarian. Some of the German shells were falling short into the pools of the Somme river and exploded under water. Two Australians spent the day in a boat rowing about and watching for a shell to explode and then picked up the stunned fish. They wore their gas masks to prevent recognition!

Major battles: Operation Blücher-Yorck / Third Battle of the Aisne, 27 May–6 June

Aiming to tie the Allies down to allow a main attack in the north, the Germans launched their third large-scale attack at Chemin des Dames and the River Aisne with a ferocious artillery barrage that shattered French units massed in the front line. The Germans advanced 14 miles on the first day – an unprecedented success on the Western Front. Pleased with his success, German commander Erich Ludendorff changed his plans and took forces reserved for the northern attack to support a drive for Paris, but the advance ran out of supplies and momentum as American troops – fighting their first engagement of the war at Cantigny – and French forces stood in the way.

2 MILLION

Shells fired in 4½-hour-long preliminary bombardment.

Your country and mine ought not to be fighting against each other, we ought to be fighting together against a third. I had no idea you would fight me. I was very friendly with your Royal Family with whom I am related.
Kaiser Wilhelm II to Brigadier-General Hubert Rees on the British officer's capture.

On to Paris
Message on German trucks.

Retreat? Hell, we only just got here.
Captain Lloyd Williams, US Marines, Belleau Wood.

Williams was killed in the battle.

THE 6TH OF JUNE

On 6 June the US Marines began a counter-attack to take Belleau Wood. On the first day they lost 1,087 men – more than had been lost in the whole of the Marines' history. Three weeks of brutal fighting eventually saw the wood taken.

Major battles: Operation Gneisenau / Battle of Matz, 9–13 June

This German attack was intended to straighten their forward line. Despite inadequate planning they pushed the French back, gaining 6 miles of territory and inflicting heavier casualties than they suffered. However, the offensive floundered and French counter-attacks forced the Germans to halt proceedings after only a few days.

War prolongers!
Abuse shouted by German soldiers to their reinforcements.

Major battles: Peace Offensive / Second Battle of the Marne, 15 July–5 August

The Germans still hoped to create a diversion that would allow a decisive attack in Flanders. Divisions drove forward, crossing the River Marne in several places, but were held. The Allies then launched a counter-attack, pushing the Germans back to their March starting positions. The German offensive in Flanders was finally cancelled.

36 PER CENT

Casualty rate of the British Fifth Army during the Spring Offensive.

963,000

German losses from the Spring Offensive.

10,000

The number of American soldiers arriving each day in France. By the summer of 1918 half a million 'doughboys' were on the front line.

207 v. 203

German v. Allied divisions on the Western Front in July.

THE PRANCING HORSE

Francesco Baracca, Italy's highest-scoring fighter ace, was killed in June. His aircraft featured a prancing horse symbol painted on the side. Years later Francesco's mother suggested to a young racing driver called Enzo Ferrari that he adopt the symbol for his racing cars.

THE TWO MADONNAS OF PERVYSE

Nickname given by Belgian troops to two British women: Mairi Chisholm and Elsie Knocker, who had travelled to Ypres in 1914. They set up an independent first aid station until injured in a gas attack in 1918. They were awarded 17 medals for bravery.

THE VC FACTORY

After an explosion at the Chilwell National Shell Filling Factory in Nottingham killed 134 employees, it was suggested the Victoria Cross be awarded to staff for their subsequent bravery in going about their work. Sadly this was not done, as the medal could only be given to individuals in uniform.

4,808,000

Number of women in non-domestic service employment in April, 1.5 million more than four years earlier.

THE LAST DECLARATION

On 19 July Honduras – the last country to join the war – declared war on Germany.

THE RED BARON

Manfred von Richthofen was the 'ace of aces' – the fighter pilot who brought down the most enemy aircraft. He had begun the war as a cavalry officer before transferring to the German air force. He led a fighter wing known as the Flying Circus because of their brightly painted aircraft. Von Richthofen's own personal machines were painted bright red, giving rise to his nickname: the Red Baron. Between September 1916 and April 1918 he brought down 80 Allied aircraft:

BE.12	(4)
BE.2c	(6)
BE.2d	(6)
BE.2e	(4)
Bristol Fighter F.2a	(2)
Bristol Fighter F.2b	(3)
DH.2	(4)
DH.5	(1)
FE.2b	(12)
FE.2d	(1)
FE.8	(2)
FK.8	(1)
Martinsyde G.100	(1)
Nieuport 17	(5)
RE.8	(7)
SE.5a	(3)
Sopwith 1½ Strutter	(3)
Sopwith Camel	(8)
Sopwith Pup	(2)
Spad VII	(5)

I hope the bastard roasted on the way down.

RAF fighter pilot Mick Mannock on refusing to
toast Manfred von Richthofen on his demise.

MRS LAWRENCE

British novelist D. H. Lawrence was married to Frieda
von Richthofen, a distant cousin of fighter ace Manfred.

OVERSEAS LABOUR

Britain employed manual workers from several
nationalities to work in France:

Chinese	96,000
Indians	48,000
South Africans	21,000
Egyptians	15,000
West Indians	8,000

540,000

Number of British Army reinforcements sent to the Western Front between March and August.

Major battles: Amiens, 8–11 August

In July Allied attacks had shown the effectiveness of 'all-arms' battle tactics: troops and tanks advancing behind an artillery 'creeping barrage' as ground-attack aircraft swept overhead. At Amiens these were put into operation to great effect.

The offensive began with British, Australian, Canadian and French troops attacking east of the city. On the first day the Australians met their objectives by early afternoon, taking 8,000 prisoners. The Canadian Corps advanced the furthest: 8 miles. They took 5,000 prisoners.

The advance slowed as attackers outreached their heavy artillery support and ran up against troops defending from their 1917 trench positions, but it had given an indication of how the war could be progressed.

A black day of the German Army.
General Erich Ludendorff, on 8 August 1918

CREEPING BARRAGE

As the troops left their own trenches to advance, the artillery barrage began firing 200 yards in front of their starting line. It then began to 'lift', increasing in range at timed intervals in a 'creeping barrage':

After 3 minutes	+ 100 yards
2 minutes	+ 100 yards
3 minutes	+ 100 yards
3 minutes	+ 100 yards
3 minutes	+ 100 yards
3 minutes	+ 100 yards
3 minutes	+ 100 yards
3 minutes	+ 100 yards
3 minutes	+ 100 yards
3 minutes	+ 100 yards

The barrage included 40 adjustments in this phase of the attack.

10 MILLION

Rounds of small-arms ammunition supplied to the Canadian Corps.

KEEP YOUR MOUTHS SHUT!

Keep your mouths shut! The success of any operation we carry out depends chiefly on surprise. Do not talk – when you know that your unit is making preparations for an attack, don't talk about them to men in other units, or to strangers, and keep your mouth shut, especially in public places.

Notice pasted into each British soldier's paybook urging secrecy – essential to success at Amiens. Many previous battles had seen the Germans fully aware of Allied plans.

95

Percentage of German artillery positions identified before Amiens.

It is by far the best fighting day I have ever had.
Lt Ernest Rollings MC, 17th Armoured Car Battalion

While behind enemy lines, Rollings recovered detailed plans of the Hindenburg Line. In 1931 a news report described the Welshman as 'The Man Who Ended the War'.

15,000

Number of cavalry horses prepared for action at Amiens. Cavalrymen had operated as unmounted infantry for most of the war – there were few opportunities for horse-mounted soldiers to fight effectively on the typical Western Front battlefield. As the fighting became more open cavalry were utilised. British cavalry captured 12 German cavalrymen one hour before the armistice.

LEANING VIRGIN

Earlier in the war, in the town of Albert, near to the Somme, a church statue of the Virgin Mary was hit. It didn't fall completely and remained hanging. It was reckoned when it finally fell the war would end. In August 1918 the statue toppled.

Dear Tommy
You are quite welcome to what we are leaving. When we stop we shall stop, and stop you in a manner you won't appreciate.
Fritz
Notice left in German trench, summer 1918

HUNDRED DAYS

The Hundred Days Offensive was a series of Allied engagements that put continuous pressure on the retreating Germans. It began at Amiens and finished on 11 November. Although the Germans realised they were to be denied victory they fought tenaciously, inflicting heavy casualties. The following battles took place in the last four months of the war:

Amiens
Montdidier
Albert
Second Noyon
Second Bapaume
Mont St Quentin-Péronne
Second Arras
Scarpe
Drocourt-Quéant Line
Saint-Mihiel
Fifth Ypres
Havrincourt
Épehy
Meuse-Argonne
Canal du Nord
St Quentin Canal
Beaurevoir Line
Second Cambrai
Courtrai
Mont-D'Origny
Selle
Valenciennes
Sambre

Major battles: Meuse-Argonne, 26 September–11 November

This was the American Expeditionary Force's largest offensive, featuring over 1.25 million troops. While the Americans had found immediate success at Saint-Mihiel earlier in the month, this attack proved to be more difficult as they faced strong German defences in the dense Argonne forest. The weather did not help: it rained on 40 of the battle's 47 days. Despite their adherence to outdated tactics that brought about heavy casualties, the Americans prevailed and continued their assault right up until the end of the war.

At least I'll get my DSC.
Colonel George S. Patton, on being wounded.
He was later awarded his Distinguished Service Cross.

200,000

African-American troops who served in France.

US BATTLE DEATHS

The Americans lost 53,402 men killed in the six months they fought in the war. In Vietnam 58,220 were killed – in fighting that lasted 8 years.

SIAM EXPEDITIONARY FORCE

Thirteen hundred servicemen from Siam travelled to France in 1918, although they arrived too late to see any combat. Nineteen died, from accidents or Spanish flu.

ONE

The number of days it took British troops to cross the battlefield at Passchendaele in September. It had taken four months in 1917.

You boys have made history.
Brigadier General J. Harington, 46th (North Midland) Division, on the breaching of the Hindenburg Line on 29 September.

The division had been given the difficult task of crossing the heavily defended St Quentin Canal, a feat which they'd accomplished using rafts and pulled lines, with troops wearing cork-lifebelts taken from cross-Channel steamships. Prisoners were captured at the Bellenglise Tunnel (which had been dug under the canal by the Germans) after Allied soldiers fired a German howitzer into it.

360,000

The number of casualties from the 1.2 million men in the British Army on the Western Front between August and November.

385,200

Number of prisoners taken by the Allies in the Hundred Days Offensive.

300,000

The number of Austro-Hungarian prisoners taken at the Battle at Vittorio Veneto, which began on 24 October. Italian forces, supported by British and French divisions, pulled off a stunning victory, which provoked a collapse in their adversary's forces. The Austro-Hungarian's underwhelming performance in the war had led German officers to describe their relationship as 'being shackled to a corpse'.

132,667

British Army soldiers sent to the Italian Front.

British — French — Greek — Italian — Serbian

Troops of these nationalities attacked Bulgarian forces in Macedonia on 15 September. Two weeks later, Bulgaria surrendered – the first of Germany's allies to do so.

CENTRAL COLLAPSE

As it resisted Allied pressure on the Western Front, Germany saw its chief allies fall away:

DATE	NAME OF TREATY	CENTRAL POWERS SIGNATORY
29 September	Armistice of Thessalonica	Bulgaria
30 October	Armistice of Mudros	Turkey
3 November	Armistice of Villa Giusti	Austria-Hungary

THE KAISER

With political unrest in Germany it was thought the removal of the Kaiser would placate the popular mood. Army officers proposed that he go to the front and die a glorious death in battle. In the end he abdicated and lived out his life in the Netherlands.

PRESIDENT WOODROW WILSON'S FOURTEEN POINTS

US president Woodrow Wilson had proposed his 'Fourteen Points' in January as a way of justifying America's involvement in the war and ensuring future peace. Summarised, they were:

Open diplomacy with no secret treaties.
Freedom of navigation at sea.
Free trade.
Disarmament where possible.
Improved rights of colonies.
Occupation of Russia to end.
Occupation of Belgium to end.
France to be liberated and Alsace-Lorraine given back.
Italy's borders to be readjusted.
Austro-Hungarian Empire peoples to be free.
Occupation of Romania, Serbia and Montenegro to end.
Countries in the Ottoman Empire to be free.
Poland to be independent.
An association of nations to be set up.

The points were used as the basis for negotiations at Versailles.

> *God was satisfied with Ten Commandments.*
> *Wilson gives us fourteen.*
>
> Georges Clemenceau, French prime minister

LE WAGON DE L'ARMISTICE

With no other option, German representatives met their Allied counterparts in railway carriage 2419D in a forest near Compiègne on 8 November. The location was chosen to ensure secrecy and no one in the German delegation was a senior military figure – the German Army high command were keen to remain distant from the proceedings to preserve their reputations. There was little in the way of negotiation – the Allies presented the

Germans with the terms and if they did not sign, the war would continue. The Germans had three days to decide. On the 11th, at 5.20 a.m., the armistice was signed.

In 1940 Hitler used the same carriage to accept the French surrender.

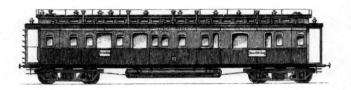

TERMS OF ARMISTICE WITH GERMANY

The armistice document detailed what Germany was required to do to secure the peace. Thirty-four sections laid out reparations and territory that had to be given up. The most important as far as most of the troops were concerned was the very first:

Cessation of hostilities by land and in the air 6 hours after the signing of the Armistice. (Naval hostilities were also to cease).

The war would end at 11 a.m. on the 11th day of the 11th month. Material to be surrendered included:

1,700 aircraft	5,000 motor lorries
2,500 field guns	25,000 machine guns
2,500 heavy guns	150,000 wagons
3,000 *Minenwerfer*	All submarines
5,000 locomotives	

Très bien.

Field Marshal Foch, Compiègne, after the moment of
signing the armistice agreement, 11 November

ARMISTICE DAY

In cities like London the citizens celebrated long into the
night. In Shrewsbury as bells were ringing to celebrate
the armistice, the parents of Lieutenant Wilfred Owen
received a telegram informing them of their son's death.

863

Number of Commonwealth service personnel who died
on 11 November.

THE LAST CASUALTIES

Almost 11,000 soldiers were killed, wounded or
recorded as missing on 11 November. The following
ones are recorded as being the last of their countrymen
to die in battle in the First World War:

TIME OF DEATH	COUNTRY	SOLDIER	DETAILS
9.30 a.m.	Britain	Private George Ellison	Ellison served throughout the war. His grave at Mons faces that of the first British fatality: Private John Parr, killed in August 1914.
10.45 a.m.	France	Augustin Trébuchon	Trébuchon was carrying news of when food was to be served following the armistice when he was shot dead.
10.58 a.m.	Canada	Private George Price	Price was advised by Belgian civilians not to leave the shelter of their house but when he did he was shot and killed by a sniper.
10.59 a.m.	USA	Private Henry Gunther	Gunther attacked a German machine-gun position and despite being waved back by German soldiers continued, being shot at the last moment.
After 11 a.m.	Germany	Lieutenant Thoma	The German officer approached American soldiers who, unaware of the end of the war, shot and killed him.

Note: the last Australians to be killed in action on the Western Front were Sappers Charles Barrett and Arthur Johnson and Second Corporal Albert Davey, who had been killed at Sambre-Oise Canal on 4 November.

Almost as he fell, the gunfire died away and an appalling silence prevailed.
US Army 79th Divisional history on Henry Gunther's death.

FINAL BOW

At two minutes to eleven a machine-gun opened up about 200 yards from our leading troops at Grandrieu, and fired off a whole belt without a pause. A German machine-gunner was then seen to stand up beside his weapon, take off his helmet, bow, and, turning about, walk slowly to the rear.
The History of The South African Forces In France by John Buchan (1920)

Full circle

As they approached Mons a unit of Royal Marines came across an eerie scene: skeletons of British soldiers killed in 1914, still wearing their army boots.

4 p.m.

Some US Army artillery guns continued to fire until the afternoon, believing the sound of nearby engineering work to be enemy gunfire.

Headline news

Great War Ends
Chicago Daily Tribune

Armistice Signed, End of the War!
The New York Times

Germany Gives Up: War Ends at 2 p.m.
New York Journal

Germany Signs Armistice
Sydney Morning Herald

The World War At An End
Yorkshire Telegraph and Star

Allies Drastic Armistice Terms to Huns
How London Hailed the End of War
The Daily Mirror

Peace!
Greatest Day In All History Being Celebrated
The Ogden Standard (Utah)

Armistice Is Signed
The Toronto Daily News

World Celebrates Return of Peace, End of Autocracy
Oregon Journal

Germany Surrenders
New Zealand Herald

War Is Over
The Washington Times

1,568 DAYS

The duration of the war.

The War in Facts and Figures

THE BRITISH WAR

1 IN 2

A British Army soldier's chances of being killed, wounded or captured on the Western Front.

58

Percentage of British soldiers' wounds caused by artillery or mortar fire.

68

Age of Lieutenant Henry Webber, the oldest soldier to die.

78

The number of British generals killed.

179

British Army chaplains killed.

628

Number of Victoria Crosses awarded.

675

British fishing boats lost to enemy action.

14,166

Royal Flying Corps pilots killed. (Most died in training accidents.)

14,287

Merchant sailors lost at sea.

192,000

British Army soldiers taken as prisoners-of-war.

240,000

Soldiers who became amputees.

256,000

Horses and mules that died on the Western Front.

956,703

Fatalities of British and Commonwealth
service personnel.

2,090,212

Number of wounded in the British Army.

7.8 MILLION

Tonnage of British merchant shipping lost.

8,975,954

Number who served in the British armed forces.

75 MILLION

Hand grenades manufactured by Britain.

170 MILLION

Artillery shells fired on the Western Front.

2 BILLION

The number of letters and cards delivered in Britain by the Post Office. The demands on the service saw the end of the 'Penny Post' set up in 1840, as the price of a single letter was raised to 1½ pence.

WORLDWIDE CASUALTIES

NUMBER (MILLIONS)	DETAILS
1	Civilians killed through military action
6	Civilians killed by illness and starvation
9.8	Military personnel deaths
20	Military personnel wounded

SPANISH FLU

This influenza epidemic in 1918 resulted in an estimated 50 million deaths across the world. More US troops died of the illness than in combat.

GLOSSARY & SLANG

ANZAC	Australian and New Zealand Army Corps
Archie	anti-aircraft fire
Big Bertha	large-calibre German cannon
Blighty	a wound severe enough to ensure repatriation to Britain, not severe enough to impair life
Boche	Germans
brass hats	senior officers
bully beef	tinned corned beef
chatting	looking for lice on clothing
Daily Hate	period of trench bombardment
doughboy	American soldier
dud	shell that didn't explode
field hare	French 75 mm field gun
Flammenwerfer	German flame-thrower
flash spotting	means of detecting enemy artillery
Fritz	German soldier
Gor Blimey	winter trench cap
gubbins	high-explosive munitions
Heinie	German soldier (US)

hickboo	a commotion, an inspection by high-rank officers
high jump	disciplinary meeting with commanding officer
hop the bags	go 'over the top'
Hun	German soldier
'in the pink'	phrase commonly used in postcards sent home meaning 'I am fine'
Jerry	German soldier
Maconochie	brand of tinned stew
Maconochie Medal	Military Medal (because it took a brave man to eat the stew)
Minenwerfer	German trench mortars (nicknamed 'Moaning Minnies' by British soldiers)
Minimum Reserve	portion of a battalion kept back from an attack to provide a framework after heavy casualties
no-man's-land	space between opposing trench lines
Pickelhaube	German spiked helmet, much prized as souvenirs
pip-squeak	type of German shell
plum puddings	trench mortar bombs
poilu	French soldier
potato mashers	German hand grenades
spike-bozzle	to destroy or disable, especially Zeppelins
stuttering aunt	machine gun (German)
Tommy	British soldier

trench foot	infection that often led to amputation
Trommelfeuer	(lit. drum fire) artillery barrage
vin blanc écossais	whisky
wastage	regular casualties from shell or sporadic gunfire
windy	being nervous

THOSE WHO SERVED

Amongst the millions who served in uniform were some well-known names:

BRITAIN

Tommy Armour (golfer)	Army
Clement Attlee (politician)	Army
Francis Cadell (artist)	Army
Winston Churchill (politician)	Army
Ronald Colman (actor)	Army
A. J. Cronin (writer/doctor)	Royal Navy
Anthony Eden (politician)	Army
Alexander Fleming (biologist)	Royal Army Medical Corps
Stanley Holloway (actor)	Army
Leslie Howard (actor)	Army
Charles Laughton (actor)	Army
John Laurie (actor)	Army
C. S. Lewis (writer)	Army
Hugh MacDiarmid (poet)	Royal Army Medical Corps
Harold Macmillan (politician)	Army

George Mallory (mountaineer)	Army
W. Somerset Maugham (writer)	Intelligence Service
A. A. Milne (writer)	Army/ Intelligence Service
Bernard Montgomery (military commander)	Army
Henry Moore (sculptor)	Army
Oswald Mosley (politician)	Army
Ivor Novello (songwriter)	Royal Naval Air Service
J. B. Priestley (writer)	Army
Claude Raines (actor)	Army
Basil Rathbone (actor)	Army
John Reith (founder of BBC)	Army
Arnold Ridley (actor)	Army
J. R. R. Tolkien (writer)	Army
King George VI (monarch)	Royal Navy
Ralph Vaughan Williams (composer)	Army
Dennis Wheatley (writer)	Army

AMERICA

Humphrey Bogart (actor)	Navy
James M. Cain (writer)	Army
Dale Carnegie (self-help guru)	Army
Raymond Chandler (writer)	Canadian Expeditionary Force
E. E. Cummings (poet)	Army
Walt Disney (film-maker)	Red Cross
F. Scott Fitzgerald (writer)	Army

Dashiell Hammett (writer)	Army
Howard Hawks (film director)	Army Air Service
Ernest Hemingway (writer)	Red Cross
Edwin Hubble (astronomer)	Army
Buster Keaton (actor)	Army
George S. Patton (soldier)	Army
Douglas MacArthur (soldier)	Army
Randolph Scott (actor)	Army
Gertrude Stein (writer)	American Fund for French Wounded
Harry S. Truman (politician)	Army
Darryl F. Zanuck (film producer)	Army

GERMANY

Otto Dix (artist)	Army
Karl Doenitz (military commander)	Navy
Otto Frank (father of Anne)	Army
Hermann Göring (military commander)	Air force
Adolf Hitler (dictator)	Army
Rudolf Hess (politician)	Air force
Friedrich Paulus (military commander)	Army
Erich Maria Remarque (writer)	Army
Erwin Rommel (military commander)	Army

FRANCE

Georges Braque (artist)	Army
Maurice Chevalier (singer)	Army
Charles de Gaulle (politician)	Army
Fernand Léger (artist)	Army
Jean Renoir (film-maker)	Air force

AUSTRIA-HUNGARY

Fritz Lang (film-maker)	Army
Bela Lugosi (actor)	Army
Egon Schiele (artist)	Army
Josip Broz Tito (politician)	Army
Ludwig Wittgenstein (philosopher)	Army

ITALY

Benito Mussolini (dictator)	Army
Angelo Giuseppe Roncalli (future Pope John XIII)	Medical corps

COUNTRIES OF THE WAR

ALLIES

Australia – Belgium – Brazil – Britain – Canada – Costa Rica – China – Cuba – France – Greece – Guatemala – Haiti – Honduras – India – Italy – Japan – Liberia – Montenegro – New Zealand – Nicaragua – Panama – Portugal – Rhodesia – Romania – Russia – San Marino – Serbia – Siam – South Africa – USA

CENTRAL POWERS

Austria-Hungary – Bulgaria – Germany – Turkey

$208 BILLION

The cost of the war. Like most other participating countries, Britain was unable to finance its own military spending and so had to borrow. It borrowed from the

USA and it was suggested this was one reason America joined the war – to ensure its debt was paid.

Post-war

We shall squeeze Germany like a lemon until the pips squeak.
British government minister Eric Geddes, 11 December 1918

'A FIT COUNTRY FOR HEROES'

... the work is not over yet – the work of the nation, the work of the people, the work of those who have sacrificed. Let us work together first. What is our task? To make Britain a fit country for heroes to live in.
David Lloyd George, Wolverhampton, 23 November 1918

The prime minister's aspirations were not met and there was much dissatisfaction amongst returning servicemen who found themselves without employment. Some remembrance events were disrupted by protesting ex-soldiers.

PIP, SQUEAK & WILFRED

Nicknames given to campaign medals awarded to those who had served. The names came from a cartoon in the *Daily Mirror* newspaper:

Pip	–	1914 Star / 1914–15 Star
Squeak	–	British War Medal
Wilfred	–	Victory Medal

THE 'DEATH PENNY'

A bronze plaque was given to the families of every member of the armed forces who was killed. Officially the 'Memorial Plaque', the 4¾ inch-diameter circular plaque depicted Britannia, a lion and the name of the deceased.

'PARAGRAPH ELEVEN – CONFIRM'

At 10 a.m. on 21 June 1919 this message was sent to all ships of the German High Seas Fleet. It was the prearranged code for them to scuttle.

Following their surrender in November 1918 the 74 ships of the German fleet had remained in Scapa Flow – a large area of water in the Orkney Islands – where they became a tourist attraction. The Germans feared their ships would be distributed amongst the Allies after the Versailles peace talks and so to prevent this, the order was given.

Fifty-two ships were sunk by their own crew members. Seacocks and portholes were opened to allow in the water. Salvage was carried out but seven ships remain underwater. It remains the biggest single loss of ships in maritime history.

This is not a peace. It is an armistice for twenty years.
Marshal Foch, Versailles

VERSAILLES

In January 1919 over 30 nations met at the Palace of Versailles to discuss the post-war world. Bolshevik Russia and the defeated Central Powers were excluded. Debate ensued amongst the Big Three (France, Britain and America) over the level of punishment due. On the fifth anniversary of the killing of Archduke Franz Ferdinand five separate treaties were signed with the Allies' opponents. Each was named after an area/landmark of Paris:

Neuilly	–	Bulgaria
Sevres	–	Turkey
St Germain	–	Austria
Trianon	–	Hungary
Versailles	–	Germany

By a date which must not be later than 31 March 1920, the German Army must not comprise more than seven divisions of infantry and three divisions of cavalry.
Article 160, section 1, Treaty of Versailles

By this article the German Army was limited to 100,000 men and to 'maintenance of order within the territory and to the control of the frontiers'. The long list of other restrictions included the prohibiting of Germany using submarines, tanks and poison gas. Many Germans saw the treaty as exceptionally punitive and it became a source of lingering resentment.

AISNE, SOMME, ARRAS, YPRES

Four bodies of unidentified British servicemen were brought from each of these areas to the chapel at Saint-Pol near Arras in early November 1920. One was chosen at random and then with great ceremony the coffin was taken to Westminster Abbey where it was placed in the tomb of the Unknown Warrior on 11 November, in a service following the unveiling of the Cenotaph. The tomb was built as a permanent tribute to those soldiers who have no known grave. France, USA and Italy also created similar memorials.

900,000

The number of men in the British Army in November 1919. A year earlier it had numbered 3.8 million. The demobilisation process had seen tensions – Canadian soldiers, for example, had rioted in Rhyl – but by 1922 the army complement was to be under a quarter of a million.

65,000

Number of men remaining in British hospitals suffering from shell shock in 1927.

A Soldier of the Great War
Known unto God

Inscription for headstones of unidentified soldiers. Composed by Rudyard Kipling, a member of the Imperial War Graves Commission. The writer's only son John died at Loos in 1915.

8 P.M.

Each evening at 8 p.m. traffic is stopped at the Menin Gate Memorial in Ypres for a ceremony where the Last Post is played. This bugle call was played at the end of each normal day in the British Army, but has taken on a deeper significance at remembrance services as a final farewell to the dead. The commemoration has taken place every evening (apart from during the Second World War) since 1928. The memorial displays the names of 54,415 Commonwealth soldiers who died at Ypres and have no known grave.

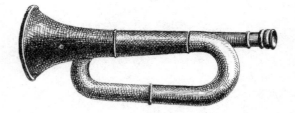

72,203

Number of British and South African soldiers who died at the Somme with no known grave who are commemorated at the Thiepval Memorial within the site of the battlefield. A programme of building memorials and cemeteries had begun straight after the war.

Memorable Order of the Tin Hats

Post-war organisation formed to provide financial and other assistance to South African ex-soldiers.

£106,000

Proceeds of the first Poppy Day in 1921. The custom of wearing red poppies to commemorate the dead and injured began in America and was adopted by Britain and the Commonwealth countries.

FLASH, FOLLY, JUDY & META

The first British guide dogs, given in 1931 to soldiers blinded in the war. The first guide dog training schools had been set up in Germany.

LIEUTENANT COLONEL MIKE WATKINS

On 11 August 1998 Lieutenant Colonel Mike Watkins of the Royal Logistics Corps was killed when a tunnel he was investigating at Vimy Ridge collapsed. Watkins had been a bomb disposal expert in Northern Ireland and the Falklands and had carried out work in defusing mines left under First World War battle sites.

£60 MILLION

The final payment of Germany's war reparations was paid on 3 October 2010. As part of the Treaty of Versailles, Germany had to pay financial compensation to the countries its armies had devastated. The penalties were controversial at the time: economist John Maynard Keynes left the Paris Peace Conference in protest as he thought they would hamper a German recovery. It was estimated the amount due had the same value as 96,000 tons of gold. Having to make the payments brought about a period of hyperinflation in Germany and they were stopped by Adolf Hitler in order to highlight the Germans' grievance. Following the disruption caused by the Second World War, a treaty was agreed in London in 1953 that stipulated the final amount to be paid and it was as part of this that the payment in October 2010 was made.

STAB IN THE BACK

In the years that followed the war it became common for the far right in Germany to blame socialists and Jews for stabbing the military (and therefore the Fatherland) in the back and so losing the war. The power and resolve of the Allied offensives and the exhaustion of the German Army were discounted.

HEERESGESCHICHTLICHES MUSEUM

The Museum of Military History in Vienna displays three associated artefacts with a grisly and important past: the car in which Archduke Franz Ferdinand was shot, his bloodstained tunic, and the chaise longue on which he died.

NEWBURGH WAR MEMORIAL

The Newburgh War Memorial is just one of 54,000 in Britain. From this small town in Fife, 76 men were killed.

A. Adams
J. Aitken
W. Aitken
A. Anderson
A. Anderson
J. Angus
O. J. M. Ballantine
D. Birrell
J. Blyth
J. Blyth
W. Blyth
G. Bruce
J. Clark
A. Clunie
D. Cowie
R. Craigie
W. Craigie
G. Davidson
S. Davidson
D. Ellis
C. Fairfoul
W. Fairfoul
R. Goodall
A. Goodwillie
A. Gorrie

R. Heggie
W. Hunter
J. Johnstone
W. Kinnear
J. Lamb
W. Lindsay
W. Logan
J. Lyall
S. Lyall
J. B. MacMillan
R. McCall
W. McCall
D. MacDonald
D. McIntyre
J. McIntyre
J. McKinlay
J. McLaughlan
L. W. Melville
C. Milne
D. Mitchell
S. C. Monks
H. Morris
A. Nairn
G. Niven
W. Pearson
C. Porter

J. Porter
D. H. Ramsay
J. L. Ramsay
R. Robbie
A. Robertson
J. Ross
D. Scott
R. Scott
R. Sime
J. C. Stobie
R. Stobie
H. L. Strathearn
H. Sutherland
J. Taylor
T. G. Taylor
A. Walker
A. Walker
J. Walker
J. Whyte
A. Wilkie
A. Williamson
A. M. Williamson
D. Williamson
M. Williamson
D. Wilson

In Flanders Fields

In Flanders fields the poppies grow
Between the crosses, row on row,
That mark our place; and in the sky
The larks, still bravely singing, fly
Scarce heard amid the guns below.

We are the Dead. Short days ago
We lived, felt dawn, saw sunset glow,
Loved and were loved, and now we lie
In Flanders fields.

Take up our quarrel with the foe:
To you from failing hands, we throw
The torch; be yours to hold it high.
If ye break faith with us who die
We shall not sleep, though poppies grow
In Flanders fields.

Lieutenant Colonel John McCrae (1872–1918)
Canadian Expeditionary Force

Bibliography

1914–1918: The History of the First World War by David Stevenson (Penguin 2004)

1918: A Very British Victory by Peter Hart (Phoenix 2009)

A Very Unimportant Officer: My Grandfather's Great War by Alexander Stewart (Hodder 2009)

Hitler's First War: Adolf Hitler, the Men of the List Regiment and the First World War by Thomas Weber (Oxford University Press 2010)

Aisne 1914: The Dawn of Trench Warfare by Paul Kendall (The History Press 2012)

Bloody April: Slaughter in the Skies over Arras, 1917 by Peter Hart (Weidenfeld & Nicolson 2005)

British Battle Insignia: 1914–18 by Mike Chappell (Osprey 1986)

Digging the Trenches: the Archaeology of the Western Front by Andrew Robertshaw and David Kenyon (Pen & Sword Military 2008)

First World War: an Illustrated History by A. J. P. Taylor (Penguin 1974)

Forgotten Voices of the Somme: the Most Devastating Battle of the Great War in the Words of Those Who Survived by Joshua Levine (Ebury 2008)

Helles Landing – Gallipoli by Huw and Jill Rodge (Leo Cooper 2003)

History of the Great War – Military Operations France and Belgium (HMSO 1948)

In Flanders Fields: The 1917 Campaign by Leon Wolff (Readers Union 1960)

McCrae's Battalion: The Story of the 16th Royal Scots by Jack Alexander (Mainstream 2004)

Mud, Blood and Poppycock: Britain and the First World War by Gordon Corrigan (Weidenfeld & Nicolson 2003)

Navy Losses and Merchant Shipping (Losses) (HMSO 1919)

Old Soldiers Never Die by Frank Richards (Naval and Military Press 2009)

Out of Nowhere: A History of the Military Sniper by Martin Pegler (Osprey 2006)

Pals on the Somme 1916: Kitchener's New Army Battalions Raised by Local Authorities During the Great War by Roni Wilkinson (Pen & Sword 2008)

Race and War in France: Colonial Subjects in the French Army, 1914–1918 by Richard S. Fogarty (The Johns Hopkins University Press 2008)

Race, Empire and First World War Writing edited by Santanu Das (Cambridge University Press 2011)

Rats Alley: Trench Names of the Western Front, 1914–1918 by Peter Chasseaud (Spellmount 2006)

Remembered: the History of the Commonwealth War Graves Commission by Julie Summers (Merrell 2007)

Report of the War Office Committee of Enquiry Into 'Shell-shock' (1922)

Seduction or Instruction? First World War Posters in Britain and Europe by Jim Aulich and John Hewitt (Manchester University Press 2007)

Shot at Dawn: Executions in World War One by Authority of the British Army Act by Julian Putkowski and Julian Sykes (Pen & Sword, 1998)

Storm of Steel by Ernst Junger (Penguin 2004)

The British Army in World War I (1): The Western Front 1914–16 by Mike Chappell (Osprey 2003)

The British Expeditionary Force: 1914–15 by Bruce Gudmundsson (Osprey 2005)

The Day We Won the War: Turning Point at Amiens, 8 August 1918 by Charles Messenger (Weidenfeld & Nicolson 2008)

The Death of Glory: the Western Front 1915 by Robin Neillands (John Murray 2006)

The First World War: Germany and Austria-Hungary 1914–1918 by Holger H. Herwig (Bloomsbury Academic, 1997)

The First World War; Vol. 1, To Arms by Hew Strachan (Oxford University Press 2001)

The Greatest Day in History: How the Great War Really Ended by Nicholas Best (Weidenfeld & Nicolson 2008)

The Old Contemptibles: the British Expeditionary Force, 1914 by Robin Neillands (John Murray 2004)

The Secret History Of Chemical Warfare by Nick McCamley (Pen and Sword Military 2006)

The War the Infantry Knew 1914–1919: a chronicle of service in France and Belgium with the Second Battalion, His Majesty's Twenty-Third Foot, the Royal Welch Fusiliers by J. C. Dunn (Penguin 1989)

Tommy – The British Soldier on the Western Front 1914–1918 by Richard Holmes (Harper Perennial 2005)

Tommy's Ark: Soldiers and Their Animals in the Great War by Richard van Emden (Bloomsbury 2010)

Tommy's War: British Military Memorabilia, 1914–1918 by Peter Doyle (Crowood 2008)

Toxicity and Metabolism of Explosives by Jehuda Yinon (CRC Press 1990)

War Wounds: Medicine and the Trauma of Conflict by Elizabeth Stewart and Ashley Ekins (Exisle Publishing 2011)

When the Whistle Blows: The Story of the Footballers' Battalion in the Great War by Andrew Riddoch and John Kemp (J. H. Haynes 2008)

Women Workers in the First World War by Gail Braybon (Routledge 1989)

World War One: a Chronological Narrative by Philip Warner (Pen & Sword Military 2008)

Websites
www.bbc.co.uk
www.biography.com
www.cwgc.org (Commonwealth War Graves Commission)
www.britannica.com (Encyclopaedia Britannica)
www.firstworldwar.com
www.historic-scotland.gov.uk
www.nationalarchives.gov.uk
www.natlib.govt.nz (National Library of New Zealand)
www.nytimes.com
www.firsttankcrews.com
www.greatwar.co.uk
www.longlongtrail.co.uk
www.thetimes.co.uk
www.time.com (*Time* magazine)
www.gwpda.org (World War One Document Archive)

MILITARY
Quotations

STIRRING WORDS OF WAR AND PEACE

RAY HAMILTON

MILITARY QUOTATIONS
Stirring Words of War and Peace

Ray Hamilton

£9.99

Hardback

ISBN: 978-1-84953-327-0

From Churchill to Sitting Bull, and from Agincourt to the Khyber Pass, history is rich in rousing rhetoric, inspiring quotations and heroic speeches from the most celebrated military leaders, writers and observers. Whether applauding great victories or standing firm against the horrors and injustices of war, the quotations and stories of this collection will take the reader on a roller-coaster ride through the many unique experiences found in military history.

Have you enjoyed this book?
If so, why not write a review on your
favourite website?

If you're interested in finding out more about our
books, find us on Facebook at **Summersdale Publishers**
and follow us on Twitter at **@Summersdale**.

Thanks very much for buying this Summersdale book.

www.summersdale.com